About the Authors

Co-author Michael MacDonald is a precious metal analyst, writer and the founder of Wholesale Gold Group.

Co-author Christopher Whitestone is a financial writer, entrepreneur and Vice President of Wholesale Gold Group.

THE SILVER BOMB - The End Of Paper Wealth Is Upon Us

The Silver Bomb

The End of Paper Wealth is Upon Us

By

Michael MacDonald

And

Christopher Whitestone

Publisher Information

This is a First Edition Paperback version of **The Silver Bomb - The End of Paper Wealth is Upon Us** published April, 2012 by Michael MacDonald and Christopher Whitestone.

This book contains the complete text of the eBook version.

The Silver Bomb - *The End of Paper Wealth is Upon Us*
An independently published book

PRINTING HISTORY
First Edition e Book version Published April 2012

First Edition Paperback version Published April 2012

ISBN-13 # 978-1475185270

The Silver Bomb ® TM # Pending

PRINTED IN THE UNITED STATES OF AMERICA

Acknowledgements

The undertaking of this effort would never have been possible but for the instantaneous flow of timely information available on the World Wide Web. This book is a sampling of the voice of the stream, as it is drawn largely from the dawning awareness of endless internet authors, editors, researchers, reporters, market commentators, traders, bloggers, and observers. These voices comprise the greater part of the balancing competition to the status quo mindset of the managed and monopolistic main stream media and are therefore indispensable in the unfettered search for what is true. In as much as is possible, the authors of this book would like to thank each and every one of them. Unfortunately, that is not practical, as the number of individuals whose impressions and understandings have contributed meaningfully to the larger dialogue touched upon in these pages is absolutely immense.

The ability to access official, particularly governmental websites has also been indispensible. Our gratitude is extended to all those in government service who seek to maintain and improve the transparency of government, particularly those who understand the essential need for freedom of information.

The authors would also like to thank all of the internet freedom and privacy advocates who continue their struggle against the on-going governmental threats of draconian surveillance, censorship, and silencing of the internet.

We would like to thank and credit every one of our family and friends, neighbors and co-workers with whom we have shared ideas and who have shared with us. We particularly would like to thank our beloved wives whose input, assistance, patience, support, and understanding was critical in creating an environment that was conducive to the writing of this volume. Most of all, we would like to thank our Creator who has endowed upon us the inalienable rights to life, liberty and the pursuit of happiness.

Dedication

to Francesca and to Lena

and

the children of all ages, to whom the future belongs

Quotations

"I sincerely believe that banking institutions are more dangerous to our liberties than standing armies. The issuing power should be taken from the banks and restored to the people to whom it properly belongs.

If the American people ever allow private banks to control their currency, first by inflation then by deflation, the banks and corporations that will grow up around them will deprive the people of all their prosperity until their children will wake up homeless on the continent their fathers conquered."

--Thomas Jefferson

"There is no means of avoiding a final collapse of a boom brought about by credit expansion. The alternative is only whether the crisis should come sooner as the result of voluntary abandonment of further credit expansion, or later as the final and total catastrophe of the currency involved."

--Ludwig von Mises

"The phantom money printed out of thin air isn't worth the digital paper it's not printed on."

--Gerald Celente

"It'll be the investment of this decade... it's only the beginning of things."

--Eric Sprott (talking about silver)

x

emergency powers to the Executive Branch, giving the President authority to fix wages and control prices. Nixon, a proponent of limited government favored what was called "New Federalism" (a belief in limited central government), and attempted to help the economy by devolving Federal power and returning block grant funds to the States.

It appeared to members of Congress that since Nixon was against more central power, he would not use the new executive powers, and it could be an on-going source of accusation that despite being given ample opportunity, the White House was doing nothing to help the worsening economy. By 1971, continued deficit spending had increased the money supply, and the resultant inflated or "bad" money drove out the "good" money as 22 billion US Dollars (that's $22,000,000,000.00) in gold reserves left the country in the first half of 1971.

Nixon then did what the Democrats in Congress least expected, and picked up the gauntlet as challenged. On August 15, 1971, Nixon, exercising the powers that had been dangled in front of him, declared a 90 day wage and price freeze, a 10% surcharge on all imports and the closure of the Gold Window. Ending the convertibility of the US Dollar for gold, as in taking the Dollar off of the gold standard, was essentially a reneging by the US on its obligations under the established order, and was effectively the end of the 27 year old Bretton Woods System.

Handing Over The Reserve Currency Baton

Named for the location of the Mount Washington Hotel in which it was held, The Bretton Woods conference was convened July 1, 1944 to find a common ground between the major economies of the world. World War II was still raging as 730 delegates came together from the 44 allied nations. It was in anticipation of an allied victory that the delegates to the conference hoped to establish a global financial order which would regulate all aspects of international monetary policy.

The actual name of the meeting which lasted for 22 days in July of 1944 was the **United Nations Monetary and Financial Conference**, but is commonly known as the **Bretton Woods conference**, simply because it was held in Bretton Woods, New Hampshire. The ensuing **Bretton–Woods System** was developed, which remained the status quo until it essentially unraveled in the 1970's with the Nixon Shock. The structure of international finance and exchange rate management was set forth in agreements made at the conference, including provisions for creation of the **International Monetary Fund (IMF)**, the **International Bank for Reconstruction and Development (IBRD)**, and the **Global Agreement on Tariffs and Trade (GATT)**.

The conference has been characterized as a struggle for control of the world's reserve currency between Great Britain and The United States. The British delegation was headed by Lord John Maynard Keynes who proposed the **International Clearing Union (ICU)** which would have essentially been a central bank for the entire world. Keynes proposed that the bank issue its own currency in the form of the ***Bancor*** to which the value of all national currencies would be pegged. Keynes' vision of a central bank included it having power to control the disproportionate economic development of any individual nation. Keynes believed that forced measures of economic redistribution on an international scale would be the end of economic inequity, which he viewed as the source of all war and conflict.

Keynes was also strongly motivated to direct the conference proceedings so as to prop up Britain's historic place of prominence in world economics. England, as being the national home of the Pound Sterling, then the reserve currency of the world, had enjoyed a long run at the top of international finance. Following Wellington's defeat of Napoleon at Waterloo, the British Empire fully dominated the military and economic landscape and the British Pound became the world's reserve currency. The Bank of England was the undisputed central bank of the world.

Then came the combined forces of crushing debt from two wars and British pursuit of interests in the Middle East, particularly oil interests, following the institution of the British Commonwealth of Nations under the 1926 Balfour Declaration after the end of WWI. England had slipped from being a creditor nation to being deeply in international debt, primarily to the U.S.

The United States had become the largest creditor nation in the world at that time and as such, carried a lot of weight at the conference. Refusing to be held to any limits on the growth of U.S. interests, regardless how disproportionate, the U.S. delegation, led by Henry Morgenthau and Harry Dexter White vetoed the British proposals for the Bancor and the ICU.

Keynes was also the strongest opponent to the dissolution of the **Bank of International Settlements (BIS)** which had been formed after WWI to facilitate payments of reparations from Germany to its victors. The BIS was shown during the conference in evidence from the 'delegation from Norway to be guilty of war crimes, specifically, that the bank had helped Nazi Germany launder assets stolen from occupied lands. The BIS had several Hitler appointees on its board of directors, as well as prominent war profiteers such as Baron von Schroeder whose **JH Stein bank** was a significant depository for Nazi held funds.

Keynes, together with representatives from **Chase Bank** argued in favor of the BIS, which was supported by the international banking contemporaries Montague Norman, who was the governor of the **Bank of England** at the time and his German counter-part Hjalmar Schacht, Adolph Hitler's finance minister. Keynes' attempt to retain Bank of England access to stolen Nazi gold on deposit at the BIS was ultimately outvoted by the U.S.-led move to take action based on the Norwegian evidence, and dissolve the BIS. Primarily due to continued resistance from the UK, the dissolution never actually occurred, and thus the BIS is still extant today.

The most significant feature of the conference for the USA was the creation of a system that placed the US Dollar, which was arguably the strongest and most stable currency at the conference table, as the world's reserve currency and the development of the exchange rate system as administered under the U.S. central bank, the Federal Reserve.

For nearly thirty years, the economies of the western world were tied to the value of the Dollar, which had been pegged to gold. The Nixon shock ended all of that. It did not, however, end the hegemony of the US Dollar. The pricing of oil in "Petro-Dollars" has continued primarily out of international habit and because the U.S. has used its residual clout to prevent any moves away from the practice of tying of the price of oil to the now purely fiat US Dollar.

The Silver Bomb

At the onset of World War II, the world's currencies were already in a mess but the British pound reigned supreme. By the end of WW II, the world reserve currency baton had been handed off to the then dominant US Dollar. After Bretton Woods, the US Dollar took its turn at the top, but in 1944 the US Dollar was enshrined as the world's reserve currency based upon the United States' status as the world's largest creditor, and that the Dollar was backed by reserves of gold.

Since abandoning the gold standard, it has been a forty year global experiment involving the US Dollar and all the other debt-based currencies that are, or were, tied to it as the world's reserve currency.

Today The U.S. is the world's largest debtor nation and the Dollar is purely a fiat currency, meaning it is only valuable as declared by law, but is not backed by anything but the "Full Faith and Credit of the United States,"

The average life span of paper fiat currencies backed by nothing is 30 years, so the US Dollar has had a good run. As the world's reserve currency, the US Dollar could write its own ticket, but now the world is looking for something more stable.

This has all happened before…only the last time it was the British pound on the decline. This time it is the US Dollar. The difference is that this time, the interdependent entanglements of all currencies is more pervasive, so the potential for damage is much bigger and its effect is likely to be more widespread.

In his 1993 book, Joel Kurtzman refers to the end of the gold standard as **The Death of Money**. Kurtzman also warned of the potential repercussions of an electronic banking system. His use of the term The Death of Money also refers to the end of the understanding of paper money as being representative of actual assets, like reserves of gold or silver. Deposits largely exceed the amount of paper money they are thought to represent to the point that many banks do not have large sums of cash on hand. It is common for most banks to require the maker of a cash withdrawal in excess of a given amount, often anything over $5,000.00, to schedule for up to five days in advance to give the bank time to get the cash.

Clearly ahead of his time, Kurtzman also warned of the dangers of "securitization," or the speculative risking of currency assets in complex and risk-intensive mortgaged-backed securities, by pointing to the potential for a wide-spread debt crisis.

These used to be separated by the now repealed The **Banking Act of 1933,** commonly referred to as the Glass-Steagall Act after the names of its sponsors, which maintained a separation of commercial and investment banking. The act was the birthplace of the Federal Deposit Insurance Corporation (FDIC). Guaranteeing account deposits up to a certain limit, the FDIC was meant to be a safety net for depositor's funds in case of bank failure. The Glass-Steagall Act was repealed by the Gramm-Leach-Bliley Act in 1999, however, much of what it had intended to prevent had already been deemed to be legal as interpreted by the Federal Reserve.

Since the Federal Reserve Note (FNR)--the US Dollar denominated currency issued by the Federal Reserve System--has been taken off of the gold standard, there has been no limit on the amount of it that could be put into circulation. Backing by gold had the effect of controlling the amount of debt that could be created, as any dollars issued into existence had to be redeemable. Since the debt-extinguishing effect of a value-backer for the Dollar has been removed, the U.S. Treasury has "borrowed" more and more from the Federal Reserve.

Following the Federal Reserve in the U.S., central banks worldwide have participated in the creation of mushrooming mountains of debt. We have entered a unique moment of history, where not just one nation or alliance of nations is financially imperiled, but the economy of every nation that is tied to the USD dominated western market is in grave financial crisis. The currencies of all nations are falling in comparison to commodities, as is evident in accelerating inflation world-wide.

Since 1971, the issuance of debt-backed currency in circulation has resulted in a parabolic rise in both national sovereign debt and money supply. The "money" most people recognized is really only a representation of a debt obligation that was created out of thin air when the loan was made. The more debt that is created, the more expanded the money supply becomes, the faster the existing currency is devalued, and the higher the rate of inflation.

Having lost over 80 percent of its purchasing power since 1971, the US Dollar is leading the race to the bottom as all other currencies join in the competition to print their currencies into oblivion. In a global game of financial brinksmanship, the central banks of the world, with the Federal Reserve at the lead, are locked in a currency war of debasement and inflation.

While the lending spree has brought the world to the incredible state of global insolvency; for the central banks, which "loan" to their governments, it has been the most lucrative period in the history of man. The banks have been the direct beneficiaries of the present cycle as they have raked in colossal amounts in interest payments secured by the tax bases of their respective populations.

It has been good business for the banks, but now it has reached the end of the road as the central banks of the world, led by the developing nations have now embarked upon a quest to obtain and hold precious metals as commodity money. The era of debt-based economy, which is dependent upon the creation of debt, which is leveraged with still more debt will draw to an end. The free-fall will come to a sudden stop and a hard reset of the respective values of all commodities and currencies will occur. The banks are already preparing for the paradigm shift.

Chapter *1*
Why *Silver* And *Gold* Have Been The Money Of History
And Why Banks Hate Them

The need to **trade** has been core to our survival as a species.

As human civilization advanced, humans have been trading with each other from the beginning. The first trades were in all probability accomplished through **bartering**, which is nothing more than exchanging one thing for another. Before there was money, as in, before anything was agreed to be money, trades were calculated and settled in units of the needed or wanted items being traded, ranging from animal skins to stores of grain. Any item up for trade is called a **commodity**.

If one thing was rarer or harder to get, it would bring multiple numbers of other, easier to obtain or more plentiful items. Over time it would be settled as to how many of each item could be traded for how many of other traded items, or in other words, things would begin to find their fair **price**, as calculated in units of each other.

Agreements would be struck between traders, and as cultures grew more sophisticated, between collectives of traders, for the exchange of goods and services. Places where traders brought their wares and where trading occurred on an on-going basis, became known as **markets**. From top to bottom within any society there has developed different scales of economy, as there has been everything from small interpersonal trading, all the way up to trades between entire groups of humanity--be it tribes, peoples, nations, kingdoms or empires.

There are problems with direct trade or barter of one item for another. The process comes to a grinding halt if traders don't need or don't want what the other has at the time and the place they come together. Mankind will always come to the point where there is need of a way to store and transport **wealth**, derived from one source or another.

The Silver Bomb

Some items of value, like land for example, cannot move from one place to another. Some types of wealth may be in the form of items that can be moved, but not easily, usually being increasingly difficult the more wealth of that item is to be moved. Some types of wealth cannot be stored long, such as fresh produce, and lose all or most of their value after a certain amount of time. Others are hard to put a price on, since some items are worth more depending upon where they are. The very same item may be plentiful and of little value in one place, while simultaneously being hard to come by and highly valued elsewhere.

Barter is limited to here and now, which compels the need for what we call **money**. It is arguably a "which came first, the chicken, or the egg"-type question, as to which came first, complex society or money, as lively, long distance trade is essential for complex civilization. Whenever money has not been available, or convenient, barter returns as the process of trade

Money is portable wealth that can be used as a way to **appraise** the value of specific amounts of other things, and can therefore be used as a medium of exchange. Its worth must be the same everywhere, so that when measured in defined amounts, it can be agreed upon to serve as a representation of a known standard of value. It should remain a constant volume and mass regardless of environmental conditions, so that it can function as a standard of measurement for the mass and volume of other things. It must be durable.

Money is a tradable commodity that is highly valuable in and of itself. It must be desirable everywhere and therefore it must be rare, or precious. When traded for other commodities, it must allow wealth to be easily quantified, compared, moved and stored. Money must be a non-perishable commodity. If it is not traded, but kept instead, it must not lose its value. Money must be a lasting and secure store of represented value.

In order to be money, it has to be able to retain its intrinsic value no matter what happens to it. It must retain the same amount-to-value ratio, regardless of how much of it is in question. Twice as much of it must be worth twice as much...half as much of it must be worth half as much and so on. It must be able to be apportioned into any fixed

24

amount, and the amount of it must remain fixed after it is apportioned. It must be divisible, also known as frangible.

All of these requirements are the sum total of human experience in what constitutes money. It was early in the history of man that it was discovered that some things filled these requirements better than others. Throughout history, items as diverse as cowry shells to bird eggs and rare stones have been used as money. These have all fallen short of the requirements as have been discovered by the tests of history that are described above. None of the above is divisible. Even the rarest of stones cannot be divided without seriously destroying its value. All of them can be subject to destruction and the loss of all value. None of them are consistent, in that they may come in all sizes and conditions, and larger or better ones must bring a higher value than smaller or lower quality ones. None of them can be apportioned into any other amount than the size or quality that they were found to be in the first place. There are places where the above items have not been desirable, and have lost their portability and therefore their tradability and value.

It was found that the characteristics of the elements that are known as metals made them potential candidates for the substance of money. Ending the Stone Age, it was discovered how to smelt and refine metals and the ages of metals began. It was discovered that certain metals are more readily available than other more precious metals. It has been a process of discovery, trial and error to determine the plentiful or base metals from the precious and rare.

Copper and the mixture or "alloy" of it with tin, known as bronze was the first readily available metal. Shortly after the beginning of the Bronze Age it became obvious that while they were not all that rare, early copper and bronze did represent great amounts of combined human labor to mine, smelt and forge it into shapes. Copper and bronze have been made into coins throughout the history of money. Iron and the mixture of it with carbon known as steel have also been tried as metals for money. Better contenders have been found.

The earliest known financial artifacts are actually 4100 year old records of civil law which refer to the amount of compensation an aggrieved plaintiff is to be awarded for various offenses. The Code of Ur Nammu, written between 2100 and 2050B.C. and similar to the more

The Silver Bomb

familiar Code of Hammurabi, which it predates by as much as three centuries, announces the standardization of units of measurement, and among other things, is followed by lists of fines to be paid in standardized units of silver.

The fines are delineated in *Mina*, which like the British pound was a measure of weight, as well as a standard of currency for measuring assets as represented in silver. The Mina was about 1.25 pounds (18.371 troy ounces), or looked at another way, the pound is about 8/10ths of a mina. The concept of the Mina, as more than just a measure of weight is made obvious by the etymology of words like *Mine*-where precious metal is extracted from the ground, and *Mint*- to coin metal into money. The Mina is described in the earliest cuneiform records to be equivalent to sixty *Shekels*, and to correspond to 1/60th of a *Talent*.

In the 3600 year old book of Genesis it is recorded that Jacob's favorite son Joseph was sold into slavery by his envious brothers for pieces of silver. Silver was known to have great value and was considered money, and indeed everywhere in the original Hebrew text that money is mentioned, it is referred to as kesef, or silver. The exact location is uncertain, but it appears that the word kesef or cecef is the primary identifier of the treasure city Casiphia, a place in North Babylonia, near the river Ahava, on the road from Jerusalem. Having been long ago raided, the stash of precious metal is nowhere to be found, as only a record of it still exists. There are no surviving examples of actual money from this era, but records indicate that standard weights and amounts of metals were in use. The basic concept of a "talent" of gold or silver permeated the cultures of the Egyptians, Assyrians, Medes, and Persians even lasting through the Roman Empire.

The striking of the first coin money is often attributed to the Pre-Phoenician inhabitants of Lydia. The treasure laden Lydian king of greatest notoriety was Croesus. His wealth was so legendary that to this day the very rich are said to be "as rich as Croesus." The treasuries of Lydian kings minted coins of gold and silver, as well as of bronze, and as in the case of what are probably the oldest real coins to have been found, of electrum, the naturally occurring alloy of silver and gold. The electrum coins were probably not actually used as currency since electrum is found in a wide range of relative amounts of silver and gold, making it inconsistent in value. Electrum coins were probably ceremonial or officially symbolic emblems given to important or celebrated citizenry. The fact that they were unearthed at only one location also reinforces the idea that they were not struck for circulation as money.

The trade of the Sea-faring Phoenicians, Etruscans, Greeks and finally Romans circulated regional currencies all over the civilized world. This necessitated a commodity-specific type of trader, the *money changers*, that kept up with relative trading values of different monies and could therefore provide foreign traders with the service of exchanging regional currencies for each other.

By the time of the Roman Empire the concept of the money changer was everywhere. The money changers treated money purely as a commodity that they could buy low, and sell high, raking in significant and steady profits by advantageous trading of currencies. Our word "bank" is derived from "banca" the Old Italian word for bench, which was the esteemed seat of business held by money changers within the markets throughout the Roman Empire. If a money changer (or in our terms, a banker) went insolvent, their "bench," or seat of exchange, was destroyed, as in "ruptured" and they were thus declared "bankrupt."

As recorded in the gospels of Matthew and Mark, the money changers had their tables overturned (as in they had their benches broken, putting them out of business) and were driven from the temple of Jerusalem by Jesus of Nazareth. Jerusalem is in what was known as Judea, which at the time of Christ was a tributary of the Roman Empire. The money changers would have had a significant presence in that day and time. The reason for this one and only recorded act of violence attributed to Jesus was the fact that the money changers had identified a vulnerable commodity market that local conditions had allowed them to corner.

The residents of Judea and all Jews elsewhere were compelled by Jewish law to pay a temple tax of a half shekel. Coins of pure silver were minted with no image of any deity, idol, ruler, or emperor for the specific purpose of payment of the temple tax. This tax was complied with by those that lived outside of the area during the three annual feast times, the attendance of which was required of all Jews, including pilgrimage by non-resident Jews to the temple at Jerusalem.

Between these mandatory feasts of "ascension" (going up to Jerusalem) the supply of temple half-shekels would be in surplus. The value of the temple shekel would fall on a regular cycle which allowed the money changers known opportunities to buy up all surpluses. During the feasts, Jews would again come from all over wanting to trade their regional monies for the only acceptable way to pay the temple tax. The price would adjust to the frenzy of demand, and the money changers would make a killing. Their activities were so intertwined with the cycle of the temple that for convenience, they set up tables, or exchange benches right in the temple. Jesus called them on their captive (as in not free) market opportunism, when he drove them out saying that they had turned a house of prayer into a den of thieves.

Following the decline of the Roman Empire, merchants from the feudal monarchies of medieval Europe still traded with each other between financing military campaigns to loot each other's wealth. The fall of Rome encouraged the northern invaders who had, over the course of generations steadily destroyed it, to continue to fuel their economies with what they could pillage. Always and especially valuable were the caches of gold and silver that were occasionally found stashed within the walls of various conquered city states or that could be high-jacked from itinerant merchants. Keeping and transporting actual money could invite disaster. Again a new type of trader found opportunity in someone else's trouble.

The natural participants in this new financial industry were those who were closest to the action. The smiths who worked gold, the goldsmiths, were already maintaining vaults where they were storing known weights of gold or gold bullion. Some of it belonged to the goldsmiths and some belonged to others and was held in anticipation of amounts needed for commissioned manufacture of gold items. By keeping predetermined amounts of the left-over scrap gold or unused bullion, the goldsmiths made more gold on every transaction. As some of these houses merged into associations of merchant goldsmiths, they became prominent in developing international trade guilds. They developed more into vault-equipped gold exchange and counting houses and less into artisan workshops. The need for safe storage became the name of the game then and remains to this day as the drive for development of the science of security devices.

It was a logical step for those among them which enjoyed the best reputation for impregnable security, for a modest account fee, to begin to safeguard the assets of others. Customers could leave for safekeeping deposits of gold bullion or deposits of gold coin money assets. These were not necessarily destined to be made into anything for use, but merely needed a secure place of deposit. It became the custom of the goldsmiths to issue warrants and notes of deposit for gold deposits made with them. These could be made in "denominated" notes that cumulatively represented the deposit, or they could be a single certificate for the entire deposit. The notes would entitle the bearer to exchange them for their recorded value. The merchant goldsmiths had become de facto issuers of currency.

The next logical step for the goldsmiths was to extract more wealth from their surroundings. As their wealth steadily grew, and it was well known by all around that they held the gold, it naturally became their business to make loans, either in gold, or in notes that were backed by gold, and at their maturity to receive their funds back together with interest payable in more gold. They began to enslave those around them through debt.

The actual gold reserves that belonged to the goldsmiths and were therefore rightfully theirs to risk through lending could be loaned out only so many times. That amount could be multiplied across the combined assets of associated money markets that could extend across borders. International banking was a necessary extension of wealth-sharing in order to bypass the limits of reserve lending.

It became readily evident that for security purposes that more customers would be willing to take letters of credit with which to do business which would promise that the final settlement was guaranteed in gold. The solution was to make loans in an abstract form, without turning over any gold. That left the gold behind so it could still be counted as reserves and further loaned against. It is here, in the vaults of merchant goldsmiths and in the halls of medieval money changers where the fraudulent world of **fractional reserve lending** was first invented. As long as current transactions never exceeded the reserves on hand and could be met, there was never a problem. Except that there was one. They were limited to the amount of gold that *they* owned.

The solution was to offer a portion of the interest earnings at stake to secure depositor's agreements to allow their gold to be loaned against. The idea of debt based on debt came into being as the goldsmiths would borrow from the depositors so that they could mix those borrowed funds with their own fractional reserves. Subsequently being provided with a much greater reserve to carve up into fractional lending, they would earn a mountain of interest, even after paying a fraction of that to the depositors whose assets made it possible. Still there was a limit to these magnificent gains as they were restricted to the combined reserves of depositors' assets. **That fact was patently obvious when the reserves were in physical gold.**

As watchers of the money market, it was noticed by the money changers and goldsmith that the price of things was subject to the actions of investors, or simply that the supply and demand of any commodity could be affected by action in the market. As originators of money lender policies, they were in control both of the supply of money, in that they could make loans easy to obtain, and also of the demand for money, in that they could contract the money supply while calling in all outstanding debt. Any loans that could not be repaid would trigger the moneylender's foreclosure on the borrowers' assets, often in the form of deposits which were the borrowers' equity which had been pledged as collateral before receiving the loans. More profit could be realized as the money merchants could gently rock the economy back and forth and pick up new clients when they relaxed lending, and pick up the assets that were shaken out of weak hands when they called the money in and shut the gates on new loans. The art of *market manipulation* has been perfected, and part of that process has been learning how to do it so as to not be noticed.

Spanning from there in medieval times throughout the Middle Ages and beyond there were potential business risks for the new caste of merchant goldsmith bankers. The populations around them, growing weary of being in perpetual indebtedness to the goldsmiths might rise up against them. They could be undermined by loss of market confidence due to scandal, or by the exposure of insolvency or if evidence surfaced of truly predatory market manipulation. The goldsmiths' only hope of survival would be some form of official sanction to deflect suspicions held by populations of the impropriety of the money changers. They actively courted the favor and attention of government. The medieval rulers of Europe were in a constant competition with each other to harness the most wealth and use it to expand and protect their interests. International trade could bring wealth from afar and Europeans had learned to look to the east, when it came to trade.

Eastern trade brought other things that were equally valuable to the money merchants, including tools of cipher and recording, as well as complex economic understandings and advanced financial product ideas. The fall of the Roman Empire had left financial and mathematical computations in the west no heir to the roman numeral of the deceased empire. The adoption of the Arabic numerals system had a profound effect on the ability of financial accounts to be quickly tallied. The concepts of checking accounts, savings accounts, and subsidiary banking institutions all came from medieval Muslim traders.

The dawning of the renaissance, first in Italy in the early 14th century and spreading across Europe, was heralded with a corresponding new age of enlightened attitudes towards lending. It was accompanied by calls from the goldsmiths to advance forward from the antiquated policies of the past and drop the profit-limiting or otherwise offensive laws, in order to encourage the lending necessary to finance the ideas and projects of the new era. This is the resounding call of bankers offered to each subsequent generation. New times call for new measures. The resultant success of the money merchants became legendary. It was not always in a positive light.

The picture of the public opinion of the wealth and avarice of the renaissance goldsmith moneychanger is illustrated in William Shakespeare's *The Merchant Of Venice* where the bard develops the picture of the red-capped moneylender Shylock, often performed as a notoriously greedy devourer of others' wealth. Shylock feels so legally entitled and protected by the law which permits and sanctions his usurious business as to demand payment of his due security which had been pledged against a defaulted loan. Shylock demands payment from debt co-signer Antonio in an attempt to collect the ill-advised and prideful pledge in the sum of "a pound of flesh" to settle the liabilities of Antonio's friend Bossanio, the frivolous and squandering debtor. The scene depicted is one of a society that has had just about enough, as it has found itself enslaved by debt to greedy money changers. Shylock petitions to be made whole with a piece literally cut off of the guarantor of the debt. He offers pleas to the court that it would adhere to the letter of the law in agreement with his strict interpretation and enforce the liable Antonio's remittance of the bloody sum. His arguments are rejected by demonstration of a "loop-hole" in Shylock's contract. The court finds against him, and exposure of Shylock's un-ethical "cruelty" proves to be his end.

Many laws were passed in attempts to limit the uncontrolled transfer of wealth to the money merchants by placing limits or prohibitions on usury, which is the charging of interest. In England, where since the 13th century there had been laws against usury, the banks were limited from getting a financial foothold, at least at first. The power of the money changers and goldsmiths would grow in locales that had lax or non-existent usury laws, and be limited where these laws were in effect. Much of the history of Europe is the behind-the-scenes actions of associations of money merchants, as they would support and financially favor governing authority which was favorable to the financial sector, and aid and abet the opposition to governing authority that was not. Governments sought use of the money merchants' gold, for the things it could get them. Money merchants sought legal favor with government for the gold it could get them.

In time, the international money guilds were powerful enough to loan to kings and to nations. The answer to the depositor reserve limit problem had presented itself and it was, of course, to seduce the deposits of the entire treasuries of kingdoms and of nations. The incentive for profit was the wellspring of the central bank. It would be the *coup de grâce* if a bank could entice the deposits of an entire nation's treasury to be placed on deposit with them. They were then in the position to act as the agent of the government, lending into the treasury and keeping accounts of collected tax revenues. It was only logical that such a bank should be renamed to reflect their national partnership and make it appear more official. No other entity would be in a better position to convince the populace and governing authority that they, the central new national bank should be endowed with the authority to develop and issue into circulation a representative currency for the banked assets of the nation.

England became the proving ground in Europe in the development of private central banks, and the model set up there has been followed ever since. But it did not happen overnight. Following the "War of the Roses", the Tudor King Henry VII consolidated power over almost all of Great Britain, and had maintained the English claim to France, such as the English foothold on the European continent of the ill-fated Calais (which would later be lost under the reign of the Tudor Queen Mary I). Henry VII died and left the royal fortune to his son at the 1509 coronation of King Henry VIII.

Henry VIII did not have the fiscal responsibility of Henry VII, and devastated the fortune his father had left him. His lavish court expenses and ambitious and self-aggrandizing palace-building programs had bankrupted the coffer. His waste, ambition, and pride would ultimately shape the end of the rule of both his family, and nearly that of all of the English monarchs. Having depleted the fortunes his father had left him, the revenues of the crown could no longer finance his unbridled lavish government and mounting war expenses. Humbled into doing what his father had not, Henry VIII convened parliament in order to petition for financing for the costs of war. He began a program of new taxes and import duties but it was not enough, and it irked him to have to go to parliament with hat in hand, and have his requests be subjected to dissent. Henry began to seek alternatives.

Finding a ripe and low-hanging fruit, Henry VIII had seized church property following the separation of the Church of England from Papal rule. In what is known as the Dissolution of Monasteries, Henry VIII replenished the treasury with proceeds from confiscated lands and in complex financial arrangements where he used confiscated church

The Silver Bomb

lands as guarantees for loans from international moneyed merchant interests. Henry VIII conspicuously enriched bankers and economic ministers who could skillfully land financing deals for the crown. Still, that was not enough, as Henry VIII needed more for his wars and ambitions to expand his realm into Europe.

Henry VIII began to take more from the economy in what amounts to an invisible form of taxation, when in 1526 and 1539 he **debased** the gold and silver currency by replacing more than 40 percent of the precious metal with less valuable base metals. This had the unintended consequence of causing the hoarding of the more valuable un-debased currency, and the inevitable stampede of un-debased gold and silver coin to other economies where it did not have to compete with Henry's debased currency.

King Henry VIII continued to build relationships with money changer financiers and created a favorable climate for them in England. The charging of interest was reintroduced to England in 1545 when Henry signed into law a decree which was deceptively named "An Act Against Usurie" (37 H.viii 9)   The act re-defined the word "usurie" as to mean the charging of a rate of interest above the level which was "fair" compensation for the risk and loss of other opportunity associated with extending a loan. Henry VIII's policy changes made it possible for the crown to make use of international money changer financing with loans that had been masterminded by the likes of Richard Cromwell, whose offspring would be instrumental in the changes of the English Reformation. The money changers took immediate advantage and set up shop in England.

The Usurie act had the effect that it basically handed over the reins of the economy of England, and laid the groundwork for the money changers, through a system of inter-connected private banking, to ensnare the nation in debt. It remained this way for decades until the death of Henry VIII. Henry left the national debt and his personal debt to Edward, his third eldest child and only male heir as his successor, who became King Edward VI, but died before actually coming of age to personally take control of the throne. The absence of an effective monarch allowed for the manipulation of the affairs of state by adolescent King Edward VI's guiding "Council of Regency." Led by an inner "privy council" under the direction of the archbishop of Canterbury, the Council of Regency, in the name of Edward, picked up where Henry VIII had left off. They seized all remaining church property, and utilizing the proceeds from this sizeable land grab, substantially replenished the national treasury.

Through the creative financing performed by merchant banker Thomas Gresham, the debt from Henry VIII's reign was virtually erased under Edward. Edward was perpetually sickly (rumors persisted that he was being poisoned) and he died at age fifteen, when his elder half-sister became Queen Mary I and assumed the throne. After unsuccessful efforts by another finance minister to tighten up the laws concerning the charging of interest, Mary returned to following the currency policies that had been started by Edward's council and employed the services of notable "economist" Thomas Gresham again. Gresham was actually an international merchant who was instrumental in the entrenchment of central banking in England. He is a clear example of generational influence held by merchant bankers over the affairs of a nation. Thomas Gresham's father, Sir Richard Gresham, had been a financial agent for Henry VIII and had been knighted for his expertise in negotiating loans with foreign merchants. Thomas Gresham was continuously backstage during the reigns of the remaining Tudor monarchs and his policy influence over the economic affairs of England allowed him to become one of the wealthiest individuals of his day.

Mary's initial efforts at reform were not successful since in reaction to her decrees, the money changers began to shut down the flow of capital by hoarding the gold and silver coin that they had formerly made plentiful. Mary's economic model proved to have a weakness in that the market was subject to artificial forces, such as collusion to withhold or corner the money supply. The English economy deflated and the money changers continued to consolidate wealth and power. Queen Mary I had married the Habsburg Phillip of Spain which caused irritation within England, making her time of rule more difficult. Together they produced no heir.

Queen Mary's sister became Queen Elizabeth I, who sought to stimulate the depressed English economy. Summoned by Elizabeth on the event of her coronation to give an answer for the poor state of the economy, Gresham who was still the financial agent of the crown is reported to have given Queen Elizabeth I a historic lesson in economics. Gresham told the Queen that it was the debasements of the currency that had caused the gold to be conveyed out of the realm. Gresham observed "that good and bad coin cannot circulate together."

In an attempt to follow Gresham's advice to counteract the debased currency, Elizabeth ordered the issuance of new gold and silver coins from England's national treasury, but did not remove the debased coins still in circulation. For a time, the economy somewhat recovered until the new coinage began to disappear from circulation. Elizabeth was not able to reproduce the feat of her predecessor brother and pay off the national debt.

The flood of trade goods from the Americas aboard European ships was dominated by Spain which during the reign of Elizabeth I enjoyed absolute primacy on the high seas. That ended with Sir Francis Drake's trouncing of the Spanish Armada which weakened the formerly unchallenged Spanish and gave England more command of the trans-Atlantic sea routes. The search for wealth in the new world was in many ways synonymous with the search for gold and silver. The story of untold fortunes to be had, and the promise of economic advantage to be gained was the wind in the sails of the explorers of the new world. The quest for gold, among other things, had launched the Spanish ships of Columbus, Pizarro, Cortez, and the other conquistadores. Many other countries sought the instantaneous wealth of gold or silver, but no other nation came close to the amount of gold brought to Europe in Spanish ships.

The Spanish were too successful. So much gold and silver was confiscated from the Americas and taken to Spain that it expanded the monetary base faster than the growth of the Spanish economy could reflect it. Since commodity money behaves like any commodity, the effect was to drive down the value of gold and silver. The plan had backfired, and arguably for the ensuing century, Spanish Traders were at a severe disadvantage as their Spanish currency was worth less and less. This had the effect of propelling the devalued Spanish coins all over the globe as they sought to chase down the value of other commodities.

Elizabeth's death was the end of the Tudor line and she, like her father Henry VIII, died leaving a legacy of deep national debt. Charles, as next in line of the Stuart Family was heir to the throne, and also to the crushing national debt that had been run up in military spending under Queen Elizabeth I. Believing in the divine right of succession and the inerrancy of monarchs, Charles I paid little attention to the economic and political voices of reason that soon came to be arrayed against him. Charles began confiscatory taxation, particularly on imported goods, to extract the funding he needed to finance his rule. The pattern repeats today of ultimately making debt public by dumping the repayment of it on the backs of the taxpayers.

Using a time-honored technique of divisive campaigning which fomented English feelings of class envy, religious tribalism and ethnic superiority, Oliver Cromwell masterfully recruited support among the common English people. Most of the populace thought of the "Puritan Moses" as he was called, as one of them, a pious "commoner," even though Cromwell was actually a landed member of the middle gentry. Being previously of no great fame, Cromwell was inexplicably elevated to parliament by a cadre of "financial sponsors," believed by many to have been of the closed circle of money lenders. Oliver Cromwell, whose inherited wealth had come from his uncle's being given seized monastery holdings as a minister to King Henry VIII, and from commerce with the money changers, had aspirations to seize the crown for himself. Taking control of the military, and forming an alliance with leading members of the London merchant community, he harvested the spoils of the "English Civil Wars" which had begun in 1642 and 1648.

Charles I surrendered to his native Scots on 5 May 1646, effectively ending the First English Civil War. Cromwell took the formal surrender of the Royalists at Oxford in June but Charles escaped from Hampton Court and attempted once more to regain the throne. Cromwell, in 1648, again defeated the proxy forces of the militarily and financially weak King Charles I, putting an end to the Second English Civil War, and in 1649 Cromwell signed the culture-shocking death warrant order to behead King Charles, thus putting an end to the royalists.

The Silver Bomb

This began the short duration of the period of English history were there was no monarchy. Cromwell was king in every way but in name, and in many ways his rule was characterized by severe social strictures that were far more dominant over the daily lives of the population than the preceding monarchies had been.

Seeing himself as the military hand of God, Cromwell began to justify his political and military maneuvering as being the express will of heaven. After military sweeps to contain Ireland and Scotland, he took the position in 1653 as the first Lord Protector of the Commonwealth of England, Wales, Scotland and Ireland. He set up the pattern for a nominated Parliamentary system which remained in effect even after Cromwell's death and the subsequent return of monarchy to the British Isles.

Under Cromwell the money changers grew in power in England setting up the one square-mile financial district known as "The City of London", which remains one of the greatest financial centers in the world today. In league with the militaristic Cromwell, the money changers led England to war after war with the French and the Dutch. War is a costly business. It is costly to those who must fight and die in its battles, and it is costly to those they leave at home. It can be costly to the treasury of a nation to finance military conflict year after year. In contrast, those who stood to gain the most from an essentially perpetual state of war between England and France or the Netherlands, were the money changers.

War is not costly, but lucrative, for those that make the weapons and machines of war, and it is not costly, but lucrative for those that loan to military-spending bankrupted nations. There is profit to be made by those that financially back war, in return for repayment with a "fair" amount of interest on the funds they lend. Cromwell's Commonwealth did not last beyond his death, but many of the effects of events during its short life-span are still discernible in the nature of international finance.

After the "Cromwellian Interregnum," the Stuart line was reinstated in a regicidal guilt-driven act of Parliament, when Charles II was enthroned. The Stuart kings like so many other crowned heads carried within them the idea of the inerrancy of monarchs and were fond of courting the financial interests when they needed them, and then turning around and biting the very hands that were feeding them. Taxation and the granting of unfair monopolies were the principal offenses they would continuously commit against the merchant class. Between heirless Charles II and his brother James II (& VII), a growing dependence upon loans from the merchant goldsmiths, which they regularly offended, began to inspire the behind the scenes seizing of control of England by those who actually held the power of the purse.

The power of the money changers was not limited to national borders. It was fully demonstrated that the money changers had the potential power to shape the future of a nation when a conspiring group of internationally-connected Nobles "invited" William of Orange to make use of the combined backing of the English and Dutch financial sectors and the Dutch military they had arranged to finance in an invasion to depose the uncontrollable Stuart King James II & VII. William was successful and became King William III through his wife Queen Mary.

William had partnered with a secret cabal of seven nobles, and the money changers in England and with those in the Netherlands (or more accurately, the nobles and the money changers had conspired together, forming an alliance to utilize William of Orange), to finance his military take-over in 1688 , dethroning James II & VII and putting an end to the Stuarts.

William and Mary were now beholden to the bankers and "allied" with the Dutch, which included the delivery into English hands of former Dutch holdings in the Americas. The formerly Dutch held port of New Amsterdam was renamed New York. This freed England up for more concentrated warfare with France which was more or less continuous. The pressures of financing years of war had created the conditions that ultimately forced the monarchial concession of economic control, and in 1694 allowed the take-over of the treasury of an entire nation, as a privately-held company sold shares in its stock and was chartered as the Bank of England (BoE).

Currency is nothing more than a tally of a holder's wealth of other commodities.   Notched   sticks,   clay   tablets,   or   medallions,   as abstractions of known amounts of a commodity, would be recognizable as valuable, desirable, and therefore, as tradable. They were all used, at one time or another as currency. Whatever the medium or element of exchange, whatever is used as the symbol of value, the truth of what makes anything functional as a currency is the level of confidence placed in it by those who use it and receive it as payment.

One of the most interesting of these currency systems is that of the British Tally Stick. It was no more than a stick carved with notches representing specific amounts of gold. It was also one of the longest lasting forms of currency, being in circulation for over 700 years following its institution around 1100AD by King Henry the First. These abstractions may have represented a piece of land, flocks or herds of livestock, grain, textiles or other commodities. They may have represented tallies of stored deposits of coins of monetary metals held in accounts. They then become abstractions of abstractions as the monetary metal which they represent was already an abstraction of relative value. Currency is not necessarily like money. Currency is a reproducible representation of money. Again, money is an abstraction of the value of other items, but it is based upon the intrinsic value of the money itself.

Clay tablets and carved sticks gave way to the easier to carry parchment scroll, and eventually, to paper.

The invention of the printing press understandably changed everything for the development of currency for the central bank which quickly found it necessary to mass-produce official and expensive looking notes of deposit to issue into circulation. This opened up a new horizon of temptation for bankers, presenting the ability to simply print "assets." The need for pre-printed notes of various specific denominations was fueled by the level of trade volume that the new Bank of England experienced. Together with the Royal Exchange (built by Thomas Gresham on his own account), the Bank of England became the new hub of international financial trading activity that soon eclipsed the volume of its predecessor in Antwerp.

British market investments rapidly became the new source of wealth, and this fueled the spread of the burgeoning British Empire.

Because of its limited resources as an island, and its command of the seas, England was destined to spread its dominion around the globe. The wealth opportunity in the New World of the Americas was available for any nation strong enough to appropriate it. The British Colonies were easy pickings in the global goal of wealth accumulation. The private, central Bank of England had certain pre-conditions for England to fulfill that would qualify it to trade its national good faith for loans from the central bank. The bank had to be given power over the money supply. The Bank was to be allowed to follow fractional reserve lending on a national and international scale. Loans from the central bank would be repaid with interest. The nation had to pledge that the tax base would be made directly available to guarantee repayment of loans from the BoE. This basic Bank of England model of central banking has been replicated in nation after nation. It was actions by the Bank of England in exercise of its control of the currency that led to the American Revolution.

The financial well-being of the early American colonies was not a priority to England and the currency of the realm was not made abundant to the North American continent. The greatest part of metal money in circulation was Spanish and so long as that was available, most transactions were settled in coins of the Spanish Dollar. When, as was often the case, no metal money was available for general circulation, necessity drove the colonies to develop home-grown systems of fiat paper currency. It was known as Colonial Scrip. It was legal tender for all debts public and private, including for the payment of taxes, both throughout the colonies, and back in England. It was maintained as a non-commercial utility for the benefit of trade and commerce. Trial and error saw the rise and disappearance of experimental regional and state paper currencies. It was learned that care had to be taken not to produce more scrip than was necessary to reflect growth in the economy, so as not to devalue it, and not to lag behind in issuance of it so as to stifle economic development. It worked very well and the colonies grew in prosperity. Guided by self-interest which multiplies to the common benefit, small local economies flourished. The prosperity that developed caught the attention of the Bank of England and of the multi-national charted monopolies such as the *British East India Company* that had inside connections with Parliament and had insinuated themselves in between England and the American Colonies.

The Silver Bomb

During his tour of duty in Europe as the American delegate to France, Benjamin Franklin was questioned by examiners from the Bank of England as to what could the Colonies attribute their economic success. Franklin revealed that the colonists had learned the secret to money and the source of the banker's lucre when he replied.

> *"That is simple. In the Colonies we issue our own money. It is called Colonial Scrip. We issue it in proper proportion to the demands of trade and industry to make the products pass easily from the producers to the consumers. In this manner, creating for ourselves our own paper money, we control its purchasing power, and we have no interest to pay to no one."*

This revelation if it were widely publicized was potentially lethal to the bankers. Since the charter of the BoE, the British Economy had gone through wild fluctuations with periods of feverish growth when the Bank would relax the money supply and periods of depression when the money supply was restricted. The Bank of England was earning millions of pounds in interest on funds it had loaned to the English Treasury and it would not do for a non-central bank controlled model of colonial economic success to point out that the bank was getting rich at the nation's expense.

The prosperity of the colonies also made them prey to opportunistic taxation to help pay England's national war debt that had been financed by the private Bank of England. England also saw the colonies as a captive market and as captive sources of cheap commodities, and passed trade restriction laws that were very demoralizing to the colonial populace. American colonists were permitted, for example to grow cotton, but to no longer manufacture with it. The colonists were industrious, and before long, the mills in the Americas were economically clobbering the mills in Manchester. Perhaps it was that their better efforts were motivated by the colonialist attitude of personal freedom to be all that they could be. Whatever the reason, their success had to be censured for the sake of the mills in England. The colonies were made to sell all cotton to England for processing, and then buy it back as English-made clothing.

It was his observation that the unfair trade restrictions and taxes, such as were levied on the colonists by England were mismanagement of the colonies as a resource that inspired political economist Adam Smith. Adam Smith wrote in his seminal treatise *The Wealth of Nations*, that prosperity lay in free-markets and what made them free was the liberty of individuals to produce and to buy and sell that which is in their natural best interest. In a critique of monopolistic mercantilism, Smith compares the natural motivation of local individuals supporting local economies versus the feigned concern for the public good demonstrated by mercantile interests.

> *"By preferring the support of domestic to that of foreign industry, he intends only his own security; and by directing that industry in such a manner as its produce may be of the greatest value, he intends only his own gain, and he is in this, as in many other cases, led by an invisible hand to promote an end which was no part of his intention. Nor is it always the worse for the society that it was not part of it. By pursuing his own interest he frequently promotes that of the society more effectually than when he really intends to promote it. I have never known much good done by those who affected to trade for the public good. It is an affectation, indeed, not very common among merchants, and very few words need be employed in dissuading them from it."*
> --Adam Smith *The Wealth of Nations,* Book IV, chapter II, paragraph IX

Smith observed that by trying to maximize their own gains in a free market, individual ambition benefits society, even if the ambitious have no benevolent intentions. Adam Smith's concept of the "invisible hand" of markets was described centuries later by economist Milton Friedman as "the possibility of cooperation without coercion."

Smith also wrote against the co-parasitism of central bank and national treasury stating that a nation obtaining loans for the purpose of war is immoral and that the ability to do so is an irresistible enticement leading inevitably to more war.

The Silver Bomb

> *"...when war comes [politicians] are both unwilling and unable to increase their [tax] revenue in proportion to the increase of their expense. They are unwilling for fear of offending the people, who, by so great and so sudden an increase of taxes, would soon be disgusted with the war[...] The facility of borrowing delivers them from the embarrassment[...] By means of borrowing they are enabled, with a very moderate increase of taxes, to raise, from year to year, money sufficient for carrying on the war, and by the practice of perpetually funding they are enabled, with the smallest possible increase of taxes [to pay the interest on the debt], to raise annually the largest possible sum of money [to fund the war]. ...The return of peace, indeed, seldom relieves them from the greater part of the taxes imposed during the war. These are mortgaged for the interest of the debt contracted in order to carry it on."*
>
> --Adam Smith, *An Inquiry into the Nature And Causes of the Wealth of Nations* (1776) Book V, Chapter III, Article III: Of Public Debts

The colonial scrip was subject to the economic and political stresses of each region it had come from and it was noticed by the BoE that colonial scrip, which was denominated in pounds, shillings, and pence, was not consistent with the British pound sterling. The French and Indian wars in the northern and southern colonies led to the printing in those areas of more scrip than was retired in the payment of taxes which led to devaluations of the regional scrip against the British Pound. Parliament was lobbied for relief as the bankers argued that the use of colonial scrip constituted an unfair substitute for the pound sterling, and decried the colonist's use of it to repay English central bank loans as incomplete restitution. Parliament granted relief in the form of the multiple **Currency Act** laws. The first of these restricted the use of the colonial currency to the payment of taxes, and ultimately the colonies were forbidden to print their own currency at all. All debts public and private could only be paid with "proper" English money, but the issuance of it into circulation in the colonies was stringently controlled by the BoE. Benjamin Franklin described the result that,

"In one year, the conditions were so reversed that the era of prosperity ended, and a depression set in, to the extent that the streets of the Colonies were filled with unemployed."

Franklin plainly stated some years later in his autobiography that this was the primary reason for the American Revolution.

"The colonies would gladly have borne the little tax on tea and other matters had it not been that England took away from the colonies their money, which created unemployment and dissatisfaction. The inability of the colonists to get power to issue their own money permanently out of the hands of George III and the international bankers was the prime reason for the Revolutionary War."

-- Benjamin Franklin from his Autobiography

The French and Indian war, or the Seven Years War as it was known in England, had left two very large things behind. One was the war debt that had been racked up by England. That debt would have been more had the British allied colonial combatants not funded their own participation. The other was the 10,000 soldier troop strength of the standing army that was to be permanently stationed in the American colonies to (officially) prevent the vanquished French or the displaced natives from renewing their threat. In greater detail, of the 1,500 British Officers that were collecting a nice fat "stipend" and would have been denied that sum if the army were to be demobilized, there were many that were of families that were financially well-connected with parliament. Potentially lucrative military careers were made secure by Parliament's policy of maintaining an on-going military presence. Funding for this "protection" of the colonies was to be paid for by the colonists themselves. Financing this standing army was the rationale of the colony-exclusive **Stamp Act** and other tax collection decrees passed by the British parliament. It was these laws that were the reason for the "No Taxation without Representation" rallying cry of the American Revolution.

The war was funded with the printing of more inflatable paper currency that depreciated so badly due to oversupply that they eventually were the inspiration for the derogatory phrase "it's not worth a Continental".

In the American rejection of English rule, the British pound sterling represented an unwelcome form of debt slavery in the fresh collective memory of the citizenry of the newly independent and "United" States of America. The Spanish Dollar had been all but ubiquitous in the colonies so the continental congress chose the currency term of "dollar" as opposed to the "pound" for the monetary unit of the U.S.

The new American nation was quite far from *united* at first and stumbled through a long process of the writing and ratification of the Constitution. While the debate and discussion was still underway the international bankers sought to set up the first central bank in the new world. The arguments about it were intense with the free market thinkers like James Madison, Thomas Jefferson, and Benjamin Franklin on one side, and the central planner statists and captive monopoly merchant bankers represented by former Bank of England employee Alexander Hamilton and the "Congress of the Confederation" appointed Superintendant of finance Robert Morris on the other. The desperate need to borrow money and the continuous threat of war ultimately strengthened the position of the bankers and the first private central bank in the colonies, **The First Bank of North America** was chartered in 1781.

Writing under a thin veil of pseudonym obscuration, Alexander Hamilton could not give the new superintendent Morris and the new central bank a better benediction when he wrote,

> *"Congress have wisely appointed a superintendent of their finances,—a man of acknowledged abilities and integrity, as well as of great personal credit and pecuniary influence.*
> *It was impossible that the business of finance could be ably conducted by a body of men however well composed or well intentioned. Order in the future management of our moneyed concerns, a strict regard to the performance of public engagements, and of course the restoration of public credit may be*

Richard" concept of "a penny saved is a penny earned" was washed away in the din and "devil may care" attitude of the bawdy, raucous boomtowns of the gold rush. Gold, which at first was free for the taking, could be carried as bullion to the mint in Philadelphia and struck directly into coin. So many coins were struck that a second denomination of a $20 "Double Eagle" was added and after 1850, coins would be struck in ten and twenty dollar coins. Millions of US Dollars went into circulation in the U.S. and all over the world, and millions more in raw gold dust and gold bullion went into circulation as well. It was common for gold dust to be the only form of currency in certain locales for decades. In many mining camps, private local companies such as jewelers made small gold coins for general circulation in everyday transaction denominations of one dollar, half-dollar, quarter-dollar and eighth-dollar amounts. The eighth-dollar coins were tiny and were known as "bits". Following the 1850 admission of California as the 31st state of the United States, a second United States Mint was constructed in San Francisco in 1853 to accommodate the flow from the gold fields and to encourage the striking of it into U.S. currency before it left California.

Much of the economic growth of this era was funded directly or indirectly by this increase of the hard money supply. People wanted and respected it as money and it tended to be kept in the possession of its owners. This was a seriously difficult time for banks. No one wanted their loans at interest when free gold could be had. The great silver finds of the Nevada strikes such as the Comstock Lode were also during the Free Banking Period and the Silver dollars that went freely into circulation did not help the peddlers of fractional reserve lending. The Coinage Act of 1857 made it illegal to use foreign coins as legal tender and provided for the exchange and re-minting of foreign coins such as the Spanish dollar which was still in wide circulation but was now rendered as surplus money in circulation by the increased production of American mining. The abundant metal money or "specie" of this period fully demonstrated that it did not require the backing of any bank or government and is never the liability of some other entity to "make it good." It can never be worth zero and it cannot be defaulted on. It will forever be "good as gold" and "worth its weight in silver."

This period of national growth saw the addition of new states and the opening of new territories into which the institutions and economic models of the east were brought. One of those institutions was the scourge of human bondage, or slavery. Wealthy plantation owners sought to increase their lands by buying up huge tracts of the best lands and exploiting the use of slave labor in a westward expansion. The financial power of slave-holders was considerable and it raised concerns among northern abolitionists that "Slave Power" was threatening the rights of citizens in the north and in the new western states. The Free Soil Party, and other voices, maintained that the newly admitted states and new lands in the western territories must be protected from large plantation interests and that it be available to independent farmers. Attempts at legislation of a homestead law to protect small yeoman farmer interests were repeatedly defeated by immense political pressure from southern pro-slavery forces. The southerners were rightly concerned that policies that encouraged the free-market economics of the west would ultimately drain the opulent wealth of slave-owners as it provided an alternative economic model to exploitation of vast tracts of land with slave labor. Opportunity was loudly knocking, as it beckoned rugged individualists, immigrants, prospectors, settlers and small farmers to continuously push the frontiers.

Of the plethora of national tensions leading to the American Civil War, the issue of States rights versus federal authority and the centralization of government was the irresolvable issue that underlay all others, and was the central topic that provided the fulcrum upon which, in addition to many others, the issues of slavery, rights of secession, economic dominance, and societal evolution were all weighed. The 1860 election was the moment that the long- constructed bonfire was set ablaze. Abraham Lincoln had been opposed to the states rights claims of southern democrats who claimed that each state was absolutely sovereign over all aspects of its governance including membership in the United States. Lincoln, who was personally opposed to slavery, had made a point to speak to southern fears of the destruction of their way of life in his Inaugural address when he stated,

"I have no purpose, directly or indirectly, to interfere with the institution of slavery in the states where it now

exists. I believe I have no lawful right to do so, and I have no inclination to do so."
--Abraham Lincoln from his Inaugural Address

The amazing growth of the United States in absence of central bank dominion was commanding notice overseas, and immigrants from Europe, Asia, Latin America, and indeed all over the globe were arriving to seek their fortunes. Lincoln knew that this was presenting a threat to the Old World debt-economy enslavement of European central bank interests.

This was obvious to the keen observer Otto Von Bismarck, Chancellor of Germany who wrote,

> *"The division of the United States into federations of equal forces was decided long before the Civil War by the high financial powers of Europe. These bankers were afraid that the United States, if they remained as one block, and as one nation, would attain economic and financial independence, which would upset their financial dominion over the world."*
> --Otto Von Bismarck

Poised to re–capture the divided remains of the United States as colonial possessions, France and England positioned forces on the Mexican and Canadian borders and began to aid each side against the other. President Lincoln knew that what was at stake was not just whether or not slavery ended immediately, as he believed that it was naturally coming to an end as a normal consequence of the changing economic climate. At the onset of war less than one month later, following the secession of all the cotton states in the "Deep South," Mr. Lincoln declared that slavery was a side issue when compared to the priority need to preserve the Union as illustrated by his statement,

> *"My paramount objective is to save the Union. And it is not either to save or destroy slavery. If I could save the Union without freeing any slave, I would do it."*
> --Abraham Lincoln

The Silver Bomb

Lincoln's search for financing for the war again led to overtures from the bankers. Lincoln asked Salmon P. Chase, the Secretary of the Treasury, to research funding options and present them to the President. Chase arranged a meeting with a coalition of New York bankers who assumed they had Lincoln over a barrel and offered to fund the Union war effort with loans to be repaid with massively usurious interest of up to 36%. Lincoln side-stepped the bankers and used the powers conferred by the Constitution to issue interest-free U.S. Treasury notes. In order to distinguish these from the many types of banknotes in circulation, Lincoln's treasury notes were printed on the reverse in green ink, which gave them the familiar moniker of "green-backs."

The frustrated bankers redoubled their efforts to insinuate themselves with members of Congress and threatened to stop payments of the sizeable campaign contributions that they regularly paid, as was then legal for them to do, directly to key Senators and Congressmen. Continuous bank lobby pressure was brought to bear during the bloodiest days of America's bloodiest war. The State bank "Free Bank" system was disintegrating in the dissolution of North to South interstate trade. The fear over war supply logistical considerations as being sensitive to potential failure of State bank financing, and forebodings of financial doom if the greenback fiat currency policy continued were used as a ram to batter a new banking bill through Congress.

During the distraction of war, the 1863 **National Banking Act** was passed which provided for the creation of the Office of the Comptroller of the Currency as part of the United States Department of the Treasury which would standardize a national banknote currency and create the National Bank System, a network of National Banks which would be chartered to facilitate financing for war procurements. The Act vastly increased the jurisdictional reach of the Federal Government through a new office which was to be the agent of this monopolistic network of privately owned banks. At each crisis in history, including the American Civil War, the central bankers have offered to imbed their services with government as the only possible remedy. The single standardized currency mandated by the Act provided both Northern Union funding for the war and a way to prevent Southern Confederate funding by consolidation through exchange of all State bank issued paper currencies, with the exclusion of Southern State banknotes.

In order to encourage the use of the National Banks (which were privately owned, like the State banks) a hard-hitting policy was begun to exact a 10% tax on all state bank issued currency transactions. This left open the loophole that depositors could write orders for payment out of their accounts if they were arranged as a demand deposit account and the vast majority of State bank depositors' funds went pouring into checking accounts. With as much as 90 percent of their assets in checking accounts, the State Banks stayed alive.

Lincoln had planned to dismantle the national bank system after the war was over and they were no longer needed. His opinion of them was clear,

> *"The money power preys upon the nation in times of peace and conspires against it in times of adversity. It is more despotic than monarchy, more insolent than autocracy, more selfish than bureaucracy"*
> --Abraham Lincoln in a letter dated November 21, 1864

Five days after Lee's surrender, just when he would have moved against the banks, Lincoln was assassinated. In what has proved to be a prophetic harbinger of future events, Chancellor Bismarck mourned the loss.

> *"The death of Lincoln was a disaster for Christendom. There was no man in the United States great enough to wear his boots...I fear that foreign bankers with their craftiness and torturous tricks will entirely control the exuberant riches of America, and use it systematically to corrupt modern civilization. They will not hesitate to plunge the whole of Christendom into wars and chaos in order that the earth should become their inheritance."*
> --Otto Von Bismarck

Bismarck had his hands full of his own country's troubles and following the end of the Franco-Prussian war, tribute payments in gold from France began to increase the German currency supply. Bismarck was pressured by the international bankers to assist in the economic exuberance following the defeat of France with changes to the corporate liability laws which allowed, for example, the incorporation of the Deutsche bank. Speculative investment during the period resulted in a boom of intense economic activity leading to unsustainable over-building in steamships, railroads, factories and cultural and social edifices. The resultant inflation undercut spending power which drove depositors to demand gold in preference to silver. The banks needed to keep possession of their reserves of the more valuable gold in order to maintain economic control. The runs on German gold lead to the banker's insistence that the answer was to remove the silver from circulation so as to stabilize the price of gold. The end of the German silver "thaler" marked the death of one of the oldest currencies around which had been the model for many others. The Spanish "weight of silver," translated as "peso de plata" was meant to reproduce the ancient German thaler. The cross-cultural transliteration of "thaler" became 'dollar" which became the common name for the peso de plata. It was the Spanish dollar, based upon the German "thaler" that inspired the United States silver dollar.

When Bismarck took the German Empire off the silver standard in 1871, the calculated effect cascaded around the world in an immediate drop in silver demand and put downward pressure on the price of silver. The U.S. National Bank System had been issuing banknotes that were fractionally backed by the bi-metallic standard of gold and silver with gold valued at approximately 16 times the price of silver. This drop in silver prices was felt most acutely by creditors who had advanced loans that could not bring more in repayment than agreed as denominated in gold or gold-backed banknote dollars, but might be paid off in devalued "free" silver dollars. By the time the price of silver had sunk to less than half of the 16:1 ratio (set forth in the Coinage act of 1834), well lubricated overtures were made to key members of Congress by Ernest Seyd, a paid lobbyist for the Bank of England. Seyd had been sent from England with £100,000 (about a half million dollars) in political contribution cash money and an unlimited line of credit on top of that, to arrange for passage of a bill that would do in the U.S. as Germany had done, and with passage of the Coinage Act of 1873, the United States dumped the silver standard. According to Senate sponsor of the bill Samuel Hooper, Seyd was the actual author of the Act. With the ease of conscious of a man who was merely doing what was asked of him, Seyd said,

> *"I went to America in the winter of 1872-73, authorized to secure, if I could, the passage of a bill demonetizing the silver. It was in the interest of those I represented – the governors of the bank of England – to have it done. By 1873, gold coins were the only form of coin money."*
> --Ernest Seyd Lobbyist for the Bank of England

In what came to be known as "The Crime of '73" the silver price-crushing effect was devastating to western mining states where silver mining was an important part of the economy. The miners and farmers who had found hope and economic prosperity under a silver standard would fight for the next quarter century for a return to "free silver" and became what were known as the "Silverites."

In the years following the American Civil War, legions of veterans went to work for the largest employers of the times which were the railroads. The railroad building frenzy was fueled by the plentiful cheap labor, and special favors granted to the railroads such as government land grants, financial subsidies, and easy, low-interest credit. Over 33,000 miles of track were laid by 1873 with a great portion of it serving no immediate economic interest. Many of the businesses and facilities that grow up around railroads, such as depots, loading docks and factories were correspondingly overbuilt as well.

This over building lead to a speculative crash when the national bank system interest rates rose in reaction to the increased demand on the money supply which had been diminished with the removal of silver. Farmers and manufacturers who were dependent on loans to offset market, or in the case of farmers, seasonal fluctuations were devastated when they could not get the loans they needed. The resultant recession was severe, and few seemed to realize that the panic of 1873, as it came to be known, was the direct result of international bank directed government policy. The formula was and is repeated like breathing. Inflate the money supply and cause a boom, deflate the money supply and cause a bust... inflate the money supply, deflate the money supply...inflate, deflate. Explain it all away as being the normal business cycle with the occasional naturally-occurring crisis that requires special intervention.

This same boom and bust cycle would be used over and over to force policy makers to shape political, economic, and social ends as dictated by the "money power," as Abraham Lincoln put it. If a boom cycle is truly a normal market development due to some favorable condition or innovation, it is actually to the detriment of the bankers. Economic prosperity carries with it some amount of inherent inflationary pressure. This creates an increase in money supply as idled funds are lured out of hiding and find their way into investments and purchases. This creates a pressure on lenders to lower interest rates so as to encourage even more borrowing, investing and spending during an already heated market. This is bad business for banks whose business is the charging of interest. When an economic boom produces big enough profits that loans can be retired, or worse, that further expansion can be funded by profit, as opposed to more borrowing, this is very bad for banks. If a boom period is allowed to continue for too long, it may be noticed that the banks are not as all important as they have made themselves out to be, so it must eventually be stopped.

The crashing of an economic boom can be as easy as to call in all existing loans and to not make any new ones. The inevitable percentage of defaults is always a bonus in the form of the assets that may be seized, but the real advantage is the flood of higher interest rate loans which may be made when the hunger for loans returns and lending is resumed. A second and more invisible way to stop a boom cycle is to keep pushing in cheap credit until it boils over. Assets are priced upwards until they are inflated enough that a correction is automatic when high prices become the cure for high prices. If the crash can be made to be hard enough, then as an added bonus, history-changing measures can be put forth to cope with the scope of the crisis.

A series of panics were instituted throughout the remainder of the 19th century. The internationally-connected, central National Bank was frustrated by the competition of the surviving State-chartered banks and began to hatch a plot to retake the economy. The first step was to remove the interest-free Greenbacks from circulation. Less than a year after Lincoln was murdered the bank lobby pushed a bill through congress. Known as the "Contraction Act", the Funding Act of April 12, 1866 was passed, authorizing the Treasury to retire $10 million of the Greenbacks within six months and up to $4 million per month thereafter. This was slightly relieved when it had led to the panic of 1873 and the implosion of the railroad building bubble. After a short recovery, another bill was passed in January 1875, called the Specie Payment Resumption Act, which authorized a further contraction in the circulation of Greenbacks to a point that the paper in circulation was on par with the gold reserves of the Treasury.

The Federal Government ran budget surpluses in several of the years during this period, but as the greenbacks had been taken out of circulation, the existing currency supply was composed of National bank notes, which were debt instruments printed by the National Bank in exchange for interest-bearing Treasury bonds. To pay off the Treasury bonds to the National Bank System would have been to eliminate the money supply, and the Bank was again entrenched into all aspects of the economy. The restriction of the money supply was the direct cause of deep recessions that swept across America. By 1877, starving rioters were setting the country ablaze as they burned idled factories and looted from warehouses and shops from New York to Chicago in reaction to the perceived symbols of affluence. Yelling "give us our greenbacks" and demanding the re-monetization of silver with angry cries condemning the "Crime of '73" the rioters protested the restriction of the money supply.

The Central bankers had nearly accomplished their goal, but full control over the money supply still eluded them. In a letter to the 1877 meeting of the American Bankers Association (ABA), secretary James Buel advised the continued and systematic subversion of the government and of the Press when he wrote,

> "It is advisable to do all in your power to sustain such prominent daily and weekly newspapers, especially in the Agricultural and religious Press, as will oppose the greenback issue of paper money and that you will also

withhold patronage from all applicants who are not willing to oppose the government issue of money.

...To repeal the Act creating bank notes, or to restore to circulation the government issue of money, will be to provide the people with money and will therefore seriously affect our individual profits as bankers and lenders. See your Congressman at once and engage him to support our interest that we may control legislation."
--James Buel, American Bankers Association

President James Garfield won the 1880 election after serving for 9 terms as a Representative during which he was Chairman of the Military Affairs Committee and the Appropriations Committee and a member of the Ways and Means Committee. As a ranking finance committee member he was well immersed in the nuances of inner economic workings. In his 1881 Inaugural address he revealed his formidable understanding of the way things really work,

"Whosoever controls the volume of money in any country is absolute master of all industry and commerce...And when you realize that the entire system is very easily controlled, one way or another, by a few powerful men at the top, you will not have to be told how periods of inflation and depression originate."
--James A. Garfield

President Garfield who had a long record both of being staunchly opposed to a fiat currency, and in stark opposition to the banking interests around him in his stand for a return to bimetallism, died on September 19, 1881, after being shot by an assassin on July 2, less than 200 days into his presidency.

By 1890 the calls for relief for the western mining states hardest hit by the demonetization of the silver and by the farmers who continued the fight for free silver had lead to the passage of the Sherman Silver Purchase Act which required the U.S. Treasury to purchase millions of ounces of silver using notes backed by either silver or gold. In a predicable nod to Gresham's law the holders of these certificates would rather they be redeemed in gold and the gold began to disappear from the Treasury reserves. Reserves fell below legal minimums and President Grover Cleveland borrowed $65 million in gold from New York Banker J P Morgan.

In 1891, it was then decided by the bankers to collectively pull the plug on the economy using the tools already at their disposal. Orders were sent in a memo to the directors of all the ABA banks that on a particular day, three years in the future, the banks were going to work in unison to crash the economy. That memo was revealed before Congress a few years later and is recorded in the Congressional Record of which an excerpt reads,

> *"On Sept.1st, 1894, we will not renew our loans under any consideration. On Sept. 1st we will demand our money. We will foreclose and become mortgagees in possession. We can take two-thirds of the farms west of the Mississippi and thousands of them east of the Mississippi as well, at our own price. Then the farmers will become tenants as in England..."*
> --1891 memo to members of the American Bankers Association as printed in the Congressional Record of April 29, 1913

The banks made their move a year early and caused the Panic of 1893 with the raising of interest rates and the restriction of credit. Millions of loans were called in and America went into receivership. So hard hit was the middle class, that it was a common sight to see newly-built houses simply walked away from by their owners, when they could not obtain mortgage refinancing. The image of the abandoned Victorian "haunted" house was so prevalent that it became part of the American psyche. The runs on the bank through 1894 were so horrific that it was still on the American mind and became the central topic of the 1896 presidential election. During the Democratic Convention, free silver advocate William Jennings Bryan gave his famous "Cross Of gold" speech which is considered some of the most moving oratory ever offered at a political convention. Jennings, who ran both times on the free silver platform lost both the 1896 and 1900 presidential elections to William McKinley who served until his assassination in 1901 and the presidency passed to Theodore Roosevelt

The Silver Bomb

In an attempt to increase liquidity during the Panic of 1907, President Theodore Roosevelt again authorized the Treasury to issue Greenbacks, but the issue was ceased with the passage of the Aldrich–Vreeland Act which provided for the private National Bank system to issue the National Bank Note. This was the test model for an "elastic" currency that would eventually be replaced by the Federal Reserve Note. All of these are the "products" of a central bank that are sold at interest to the American people.

Centralized control is the anti-thesis of free-market capitalism, and its inevitable trend is towards the enslavement of the masses by the few. It is the threat of consolidation of power that is the ticking time bomb of unrestricted capitalism. Anti-trust laws, such as the now-repealed Glass-Steagall act created barriers to unfair conflicts of interest caused by the mixing of markets in attempts to spread risk and sweep profits. Only local markets are free.

Money as a commodity can, and has at times been in short supply, and may not be available to people everywhere and at all times. Throughout history this has often required that trades be accomplished in a return to barter, the items being traded without the use of other forms of money, except as they are calculated in units of other commodity items. The recurring cycle of natural market forces is for a suitable commodity to rise to the top as the best store of value, and therefore be treated as money.

Gold and silver have both survived the test of time, which is the truest test of fitness as money, and have helped people preserve wealth for 4,000 years or more.

Chapter *2*

Flexible Standards and the Fed
The Federal Reserve...the elephant in the room no one wants to acknowledge

"Centralization Of Credit In The Banks Of The State, By Means Of A National Bank With State Capital And An Exclusive Monopoly"
--Fifth Plank of the Communist Manifesto, Karl Marx 1848

The Federal Reserve System is privately owned, and is accountable to no one.

There remains a significant segment of society that has not gotten the above memo, so for their sake, let's take a look at the 12 Federal Reserve Banks, which make up the Federal Reserve System.

It has been rightly said that, "The Federal Reserve is no more **Federal** than **Federal Express**." The usual intended meaning being that like the shipping giant, the shrewdly-named Federal Reserve is not a government agency, but a private company. It was given its government agency image invoking name to obscure to the public that it is a Corporation. It is not a publicly traded corporation, however, and its privately held stock is owned by the 12 individual regional Federal Reserve Banks that together comprise the Federal Reserve System. It is a *banking cartel* that is owned by its shareholding members. No Federal agency sells shares in its ownership, demonstrating that the shareholder-owned Fed is a privately-held corporation. The individual regional Banks are likewise, in turn, privately held corporations. In order for other banks to do business with the Fed, they must own a never-disclosed amount of stock in the Federal Reserve. Some part of those shares is held by the foreign central banks of all other nations that do business with the Federal Reserve. It is banks, both foreign and domestic, that own the central bank. As to which banks own how many shares, we may never know, since the amount of shares purchased and their ownership are both kept secret.

The Frequently Asked Questions page of the official Federal Reserve website does not help to clarify who exactly owns the Federal Reserve in its statement,

> *"THE TWELVE REGIONAL FEDERAL RESERVE BANKS, WHICH WERE ESTABLISHED BY CONGRESS AS THE OPERATING ARMS OF THE NATION'S CENTRAL BANKING SYSTEM, ARE ORGANIZED MUCH LIKE PRIVATE CORPORATIONS--POSSIBLY LEADING TO SOME CONFUSION ABOUT "OWNERSHIP." FOR EXAMPLE, THE RESERVE BANKS ISSUE SHARES OF STOCK TO MEMBER BANKS. HOWEVER, OWNING RESERVE BANK STOCK IS QUITE DIFFERENT FROM OWNING STOCK IN A PRIVATE COMPANY. THE RESERVE BANKS ARE NOT OPERATED FOR PROFIT, AND OWNERSHIP OF A CERTAIN AMOUNT OF STOCK IS, BY LAW, A CONDITION OF MEMBERSHIP IN THE SYSTEM. THE STOCK MAY NOT BE SOLD, TRADED, OR PLEDGED AS SECURITY FOR A LOAN; DIVIDENDS ARE, BY LAW, 6 PERCENT PER YEAR."*

The problem with comparisons of the Fed with any other private corporation is that, by statute, the Federal Reserve enjoys a total monopoly in its place as the only central bank. It is ensured by law that buying its shares is a mandatory condition of doing business with it. It has no competition and it sets its own market conditions.

While the Government Accountability Office (GAO) has the official onus of audits of the Fed, it is utterly hamstringed in its capacity to do so. The laws are rigged to give the Federal Reserve a level of secrecy that the military could only hope for. Specifically, The Government Accounting Office does not have complete access to all aspects of the Federal Reserve System. The law excludes the following areas from GAO inspections:

(1) TRANSACTIONS FOR OR WITH A FOREIGN CENTRAL BANK, GOVERNMENT OF A FOREIGN COUNTRY, OR NON-PRIVATE INTERNATIONAL FINANCING ORGANIZATION;

(2) DELIBERATIONS, DECISIONS, OR ACTIONS ON MONETARY POLICY MATTERS, INCLUDING DISCOUNT WINDOW OPERATIONS, RESERVES OF MEMBER BANKS, SECURITIES CREDIT, INTEREST ON DEPOSITS, OPEN MARKET OPERATIONS;

(3) TRANSACTIONS MADE UNDER THE DIRECTION OF THE FEDERAL OPEN MARKET COMMITTEE; OR

(4) A PART OF A DISCUSSION OR COMMUNICATION AMONG OR BETWEEN MEMBERS OF THE BOARD OF GOVERNORS AND OFFICERS AND EMPLOYEES OF THE FEDERAL RESERVE SYSTEM RELATED TO ITEMS. From: (31 USCA §714)

When called to testify in 1993 before a House sub-committee on the reason for the restrictions on GAO access, Wayne D. Angell, then a member of the Federal Reserve Board of Governors, said,

> *"By excluding these areas, the [1978] Act attempts to balance the need for public accountability of the Federal Reserve through GAO audits against the need to insulate the central bank's monetary policy functions from short-term political pressures and to ensure that foreign central banks and governmental entities can transact business in the U.S. financial markets through the Federal Reserve on a confidential basis."*

When asked about a bill that would lift the constraints placed on the GAO's audit authority over the Federal Reserve and would mandate the timely delivery of the minutes and video of such audits to Congress, Angell related that it is not important to know about such unnecessary things that may, if revealed, scare away the Fed's foreign customers when he stated,

"The benefits, if any, of broadening the GAO's authority into the areas of monetary policy and transactions with foreign official entities would be small...In this environment, the contribution that a GAO audit would make to the active public discussion of the conduct of monetary policy is not likely to outweigh the disadvantages of expanding GAO audit authority in this area."

--From H.R. 28: "Federal Reserve Accountability Act of 1993," Hearing before the Subcommittee on Domestic Monetary Policy [House], October 27, 1993, U.S. Government Printing Office, Serial no. 103-86.

The GAO is prevented from audits of Fed transactions with or for government financing organizations, or with foreign central banks, or any transactions made under the direction of the Federal Open Market Committee which is described on the Fed website as follows:

> *"A MAJOR COMPONENT OF THE SYSTEM IS THE FEDERAL OPEN MARKET COMMITTEE (FOMC), WHICH IS MADE UP OF THE MEMBERS OF THE BOARD OF GOVERNORS, THE PRESIDENT OF THE FEDERAL RESERVE BANK OF NEW YORK, AND PRESIDENTS OF FOUR OTHER FEDERAL RESERVE BANKS, WHO SERVE ON A ROTATING BASIS. THE FOMC OVERSEES OPEN MARKET OPERATIONS, WHICH IS THE MAIN TOOL USED BY THE FEDERAL RESERVE TO INFLUENCE MONEY MARKET CONDITIONS AND THE GROWTH OF MONEY AND CREDIT."*

Sort of like the Security Council of the United Nations, the FOMC has permanent and revolving members. To be accurate, it is the Board of Governors plus one permanent regional member that is the president of the New York Federal Reserve Bank, and four which revolve from the other 11 Regional Reserve banks.

The GAO is further restricted from looking into any internal monetary policy at the Fed and it is not privy to any communication from any member of the Federal Reserve's Board of Governors, or any employee about any of these transactions. The Fed website attempts to allay any fears that the Fed operates without oversight by claiming multiple layers of audits.

The Board of Governors, the Federal Reserve Banks, and the Federal Reserve System as a whole are all subject to several levels of audit and review. Under the Federal Banking Agency Audit Act (enacted in 1978 as Public Law 95-320), which authorizes the Comptroller General of the United States to audit the Federal Reserve System, the Government Accountability Office (GAO) has conducted numerous reviews of Federal Reserve activities.

By the 1978 statute the GAO is authorized (it does not say it is required) to audit the Federal Reserve System. The stone wall of restrictions on GAO audits of the Fed renders this "level of audit" to be mere theatrical chicanery, the only purpose of which is to provide an apparition of the assurance of oversight where there is none. It matters not how many security checks around the perimeter of the fed the GAO does if it never is allowed to open up the gates of that stone wall and investigate the true nature of matters on the inside.

The Fed webpage quoted above also describes layers of internal audit conducted by the Fed Board on itself. We are told that:

> "IN ADDITION, THE **BOARD'S OFFICE OF INSPECTOR GENERAL (OIG)** AUDITS AND INVESTIGATES **BOARD** PROGRAMS AND OPERATIONS AS WELL AS THOSE **BOARD** FUNCTIONS DELEGATED TO THE **RESERVE BANKS** COMPLETED AND ACTIVE GAO REVIEWS AND COMPLETED OIG AUDITS, REVIEWS AND ASSESSMENTS ARE LISTED IN THE BOARD'S ANNUAL REPORT (BEFORE 2002, THE REVIEWS WERE LISTED IN THE BOARD'S ANNUAL REPORT: BUDGET REVIEW)."(emphasis added)

Not to leave the door open to criticism that these internal audits may be prone to what may be diplomatically referred to as "inaccuracies," we are further informed that the Board's internal audits are looked over by an "independent outside auditor".

> "THE BOARD'S FINANCIAL STATEMENTS, AND ITS COMPLIANCE WITH LAWS AND REGULATIONS AFFECTING THOSE STATEMENTS, ARE AUDITED ANNUALLY BY AN OUTSIDE AUDITOR RETAINED BY THE OIG. THE FINANCIAL STATEMENTS OF THE RESERVE BANKS ARE ALSO AUDITED ANNUALLY BY AN INDEPENDENT OUTSIDE AUDITOR."

The independent outside auditor is contracted annually, not by the government but by the Fed Board itself. With trillions on the table, it is fairly easy to guess that the Fed Board would want to hire firms whose findings would be favorable toward the central bank. It is the services of the likes of **Coopers and Lybrand** and **Price Waterhouse** that produced many of the legitimizing blessings over the Fed's internal oversight like this rubber stamp from Price Waterhouse which was delivered to be included in the Board's 1996 Annual Report (nearly identical ones appear in other Annual Reports):

> "We have audited the accompanying balance sheets of the Board of Governors of the Federal Reserve System (the Board) as of December 31, 1995 and 1994, and the

related statements of revenues and expenses for the years then ended. These financial statements are the responsibility of the Board's management. ***Our responsibility is to express an opinion on these financial statements based on our audits.***

We conducted our audits in accordance with generally accepted accounting standards and Government Accounting Standards issued by the Comptroller General of the United States. Those standards require that we plan and perform the audits to obtain reasonable assurance about whether the financial statements are free of material misstatement. An audit includes examining, on a test basis, evidence supporting the amounts and disclosures in the financial statements. An audit also includes assessing the accounting principles used and significant estimates made by management, as well as evaluating the overall financial statement presentation. We believe that our audits provide a reasonable basis for our opinion.

In our opinion the financial statements referred to above present fairly, in all material respects, the financial position of the Board as of December 31, 1995 and 1994, and the results of its operations and its cash flows for the years then ended in conformity with generally accepted accounting principles.

As discussed in Notes 1 and 3 to the financial statements, the Board implemented Statement of Financial Accounting Standards No. 112, Employers' Accounting for Postemployment Benefits, effective January 1, 1994. In accordance with Government Accounting Standards, we have also issued a report dated March 25, 1996 on our consideration of the Board's internal control structure and a report dated March 25, 1996 on its compliance with laws and regulations."(emphasis added)

The Board is also required by law to deliver an annual report to the Speaker of the House of Representatives, and to report twice a year to Congressional Banking committees, and to testify before Congress whenever requested. The information in these reports to Congress is of dubious value, considering the above mentioned areas of Fed activity that are beyond scrutiny.

Basically, anything the Federal Reserve does which is hidden in the above exclusions can ultimately be called an internal Board policy secret that cannot be looked into. That is, without a change in the current statute. Again, from the Fed's own website

> *"THE FEDERAL RESERVE'S ULTIMATE ACCOUNTABILITY IS TO CONGRESS, WHICH AT ANY TIME CAN AMEND THE FEDERAL RESERVE ACT." (emphasis added)*

Characterized as necessary to national economic security, the secrecy of the Fed was assured in 1993 when then President Bill Clinton rejected bi-partisan H.R. 28: "Federal Reserve Accountability Act of 1993," legislation that would have allowed Congress to get a peek at the inner workings of the central bank system. Clinton's argument was that Fed audit reforms would "run the risk of undermining market confidence in the Fed."

This statement is one of a long line of pro-bank double-speak, for it is impossible that more transparency equals less confidence, but the other way around. Upon inspection, this statement looks more and more like another in a long line of Freudian slip admissions of closeted skeletal remains, which if brought to light, would shock and horrify.

After the Crash of 2008, the calls for auditing the Federal Reserve have re-intensified. Congressman Ron Paul (R-TX) sponsored the "Audit the Fed "bill HR1207 in the House of Representatives, and in the Senate, Bernie Sanders sponsored its companion bill S604, together with 32 co-sponsors which would have amended the code to remove the restrictions on the GAO audits of the Federal Reserve, and mandated a full audit. The bill had 319 co-sponsors in the House, with wide bi-partisan support, including Lynn Woolsey (D-CA), co-chair of the Progressive Caucus; Stephanie Sandlin (D-SD), chair of the Blue Dog Coalition;, and Pete Sessions (R-TX), chair of the Republican Congressional Campaign Committee.

During proceedings of the House Committee on Oversight and Government Reform hearings, under questioning from Representative

John Duncan (R-TN), Federal Reserve chairman Ben Bernanke, who in February of 2006 had taken over the helm of the Fed from retiring chairman Alan Greenspan, drew the following line in the sand,

> *"My concern about the legislation is that if the GAO is auditing not only the operational aspects of our programs and the details of the programs but is making judgments about our policy decisions, that would effectively be a takeover of monetary policy by the Congress, a repudiation of the independence of the Federal Reserve which would be highly destructive to the stability of the financial system, the Dollar and our national economic situation."*
> --Testimony of Ben S. Bernanke before the House Thursday Jun 25, 2009 http://oversight.house.gov/

Bernanke's implication was un-mistakable. If the Federal Reserve was opened up for all to see, and its policies were to actually face congressional oversight, the result would be the repudiated Fed's destruction of the economy. Bernanke called such oversight a "take-over" of monetary policy by Congress. Perhaps Mr. Bernanke believed that the powers granted to Congress in the U.S. Constitution are irrelevant. From Article1; Section 8; Clauses 1-6:

"SECTION 8.

CLAUSE 1: THE CONGRESS SHALL HAVE POWER TO LAY AND COLLECT TAXES, DUTIES, IMPOSTS AND EXCISES, TO PAY THE DEBTS AND PROVIDE FOR THE COMMON DEFENSE AND GENERAL WELFARE OF THE UNITED STATES; BUT ALL DUTIES, IMPOSTS AND EXCISES SHALL BE UNIFORM THROUGHOUT THE UNITED STATES;
CLAUSE 2: TO BORROW MONEY ON THE CREDIT OF THE UNITED STATES;
CLAUSE 3: TO REGULATE COMMERCE WITH FOREIGN NATIONS, AND AMONG THE SEVERAL STATES, AND WITH THE INDIAN TRIBES;
CLAUSE 4: TO ESTABLISH AN UNIFORM RULE OF NATURALIZATION, AND UNIFORM LAWS ON THE SUBJECT OF BANKRUPTCIES THROUGHOUT THE UNITED STATES;
CLAUSE 5: TO COIN MONEY, REGULATE THE VALUE THEREOF, AND OF FOREIGN COIN, AND FIX THE STANDARD OF WEIGHTS AND MEASURES;

CLAUSE 6: TO PROVIDE FOR THE PUNISHMENT OF COUNTERFEITING THE SECURITIES AND CURRENT COIN OF THE UNITED STATES;"

Perhaps it is the above Clause 6 that Mr. Bernanke should be most afraid of.

HR1207 was passed in the House of Representatives, but fell in the Senate to overwhelming pressure from the Obama administration and the Fed.

It was starkly revealing that a movement to audit the fed which was finding a growing majority in both Houses of Congress was so vigorously stifled by the entrenched banking interests. The pressures exerted on Senate lawmakers were related in the following article that appeared in the online Wall Street Journal.

MAY 7, 2010

PLAN FOR CONGRESSIONAL AUDITS OF FED DIES IN SENATE
By SUDEEP REDDY and MICHAEL R. CRITTENDEN

Last-minute maneuvering in the Senate allowed the Federal Reserve to sidestep legislation that would have exposed its interest-rate decision-making to congressional auditors.

Pressure from the Obama administration led Senate lawmakers to alter a provision pushed by Sen. Bernie Sanders (I., Vt.) that was gaining momentum despite opposition from the Treasury and the Fed. It would have largely repealed a 32-year-old law that shields Fed monetary policy from congressional auditors.

European Pressphoto Agency Sen. Bernie Sanders of Vermont

The Silver Bomb

The compromise, endorsed by Senate Banking Committee Chairman Christopher Dodd (D., Conn.) and the Treasury would require the Fed to disclose more details about its lending during the financial crisis. It would also require a one-time audit of those loans and a one-time review of Fed governance. A formal vote was pushed back until next week.

Thursday's Senate showdown came after senators on the left and right joined forces to support Mr. Sanders' provision.

"At a time when our entire financial system almost collapsed, we cannot let the Fed operate in secrecy any longer," Mr. Sanders said. "The American people have a right to know."

But Fed Chairman Ben Bernanke, while insisting on a commitment to "openness" at the Fed, said in a letter to Congress the Sanders measure would "seriously threaten monetary policy independence, increase inflation fears and market interest rates, and damage economic stability and job creation."

Deputy Treasury Secretary Neal Wolin, in a statement, endorsed the revisions to the Sanders provision, saying they would provide a comprehensive audit of the Federal Reserve Board's operations in response to the financial crisis, "while preserving the existing protections of the Federal Reserve's independence with respect to monetary policy."

A House bill sponsored by Rep. Ron Paul (R., Texas) that passed in December contains a proposal similar to the original Sanders measure. If the Senate bill passes, it will need to be reconciled in a conference committee. That keeps the pressure on the Fed alive for the coming months.

The original Sanders measure stated that it shouldn't be "construed as interference in or dictation of monetary policy." But the Fed and administration warned that would allow auditors to interview Fed policy makers and staffers about monetary policy, thereby allowing congressional critics to pressure the Fed and undermine its independence.

Like most other capitalist democracies, U.S. politicians have given the central bank considerable latitude to control interest rates on the theory that elected politicians are prone to keep rates too low to get more growth during their terms at the cost of more inflation later. Although sponsors of legislation insisted that wasn't their intent, the Fed and its allies said otherwise.

"It's a chilling kind of circumstance," former Fed Chairman Paul Volcker, an Obama adviser, said in an interview. "The more you have no clear boundaries about what's appropriate and what's inappropriate, you castrate the decision-making process. That's true for any organization, but it's particularly true when you get into the sensitivities of monetary policy that can generate speculative waves in financial markets and speculation in people's minds," said Mr. Volcker, who also urged lawmakers to eliminate the audit provision.

Anil Kashyap, an economist at the University of Chicago's Booth School of Business, stressed that independent central banks need to be insulated from politics and make decisions several months ahead of expected trends.

"There are times when you have to start raising interest rates before the economy's recovering. If you're going to get audited while you do that, you know you're going to be slower—meaning we're going to tolerate higher inflation."

Before the last-minute compromise, the Fed's foes appeared to be winning, and got a major boost when Senate Majority Leader Harry Reid (D., Nev.) said he would side with Mr. Sanders.

Mr. Bernanke, meanwhile, returned to Washington Thursday afternoon after a morning speech in Chicago to continue pressing for changes to the Sanders bill. In the past few days, Mr. Bernanke has spoken to at least a half-dozen senators to argue the Fed's case that the bill would deeply damage the Fed's credibility and ability to make tough decisions about interest rates.

At least half a dozen Obama administration officials joined the blitz, including Treasury Secretary Timothy Geithner—a former Fed official—and Rahm Emanuel, the White House chief of staff. Administration aides credited Mr. Dodd with pushing back against the original amendment and developing an acceptable alternative.

New York Fed President William Dudley also advocated to scale back the scope of the auditing. He was among those arguing that ongoing reviews of the Fed's regular lending to financial institutions would stigmatize the program and cripple the Fed's role as the nation's lender of last resort.

The Senate beat back another amendment with populist tinges, defeating 61-33 a provision that would have put strict caps on the size of the nation's banks. Offered by a bloc of liberal Democrats, it would have capped at 10% the limit on the nation's total insured deposits any single bank holding company could carry. It would have also set a 6% leverage limit for banks and capped their non-deposit liabilities at 2% of U.S. gross domestic product.
—Damian Paletta, Jonathan Weisman and Jon Hilsenrath contributed to this article.

It is amazing how utterly blind the bank cartel mouthpieces like Fed Chairman Ben Bernanke are to how their arrogance plays off to the American people. In the WSJ article above, Bernanke warns of the dire consequences of Congressional peering behind the curtain into the Fed where he is quoted as saying that the Sanders bill would,

"seriously threaten monetary policy independence"

His complaint is that some of the free-reign of the unfettered central bank might be curtailed, *which coincidentally, is exactly what the bill called for.* Considering the massive currency printing euphemistically referred to as Quantitative Easing II (QE-2) and the

Fed's promise to stick to zero to negative interest rates at the discount window, both of which followed the torpedoing of this bill and both of which are guaranteed to result in further inflation, it is quite laughable for Bernanke to have threatened economic Armageddon by adding that to take a look into the Fed would,

> *"increase inflation fears and market interest rates, and damage economic stability and job creation."*

This is as accurate as anyone could have described the scenario which has, with or without audit oversight of the Fed, unfolded in the meantime.

The Federal Reserve receives no budget for its activities, and as such is beyond the reach of congressional purse strings. It is entirely autonomous, and shielded from scrutiny by a cloak of pro-banking cultural bias, and legal entitlement.

The Fed is an unchallenged oligarchy of the banking elite. It operates more like a monarchy than a part of any national interest.

The Chairman of the Board of Governors of the Federal Reserve serves for a Presidential Administration eclipsing term of 14 years, and is appointed by the President of the United States. The appointee is however, from a short list of heirs-apparent that has been provided by the Fed Board of Governors to the President, as if the President is merely officiating at the coronation of the named successor of a departed monarch.

The Federal Reserve System is supposed to be a not-for-profit institution. For any private company, profit is the prime incentive for all policy, and so it is for the 12 Federal Reserve Banks. The difference is the profit created by Fed policy is actually interest paid on the national debt **($454,393,280,417.03 for fiscal 2011 alone)** which does not go directly to the Fed, but to the private banks (including share-holding member banks), foreign governments, corporations, and wealthy individuals that own it in the form of US Debt instruments or securities including Treasury Bills, Notes, Bonds, TIPS, US Savings Bonds and State and Local Government Series securities.

These US Bonds are purchased from the Federal Reserve at regular auction, which is issued them in payment for the US Dollars that the Fed has created for the US Treasury Bureau of Public Debt. The Treasury Bureau does not have any public policy decision-making authority but is reacting to the demands of the Budget of the United States and Federal expenditures such as for emergency spending measures and other off-budget spending, including presumably the release into circulation of stimulus funding as deemed necessary by the Fed's secretive "security council," the FOMC.

The Fed mostly creates US Dollars electronically out of thin air, but also prints circulation-ready stockpiles of representative Federal Reserve Notes (FRN's) actually costing the taxpayer further for printing expenses, paper, and ink. It is the vast sums of electronic currency manufactured by the Fed that represent the greatest portion of the National debt. The Fed has had the capacity to do this since the installation of computer systems beginning with the first systems administered by a younger IBM systems programmer Alan Greenspan, who has ostensibly used aspects of his own software creations while he took his turn as Fed Chairman.

The money from the bond sales, mostly to foreign governments, as well as the interest on loans made by the Fed and the interest on US Bond debt still held or owned by the Fed is all part of the invisible inner workings at the Fed. So is the legally mandated 6 percent per annum dividend, which is paid on the untold value of each individual share in the Corporation to a yet unidentified list of Fed stockholders.

This provides a layer of detachment and anonymity that has thrown many a watchdog off the scent of which way the money went. Even direct questioning by Congress gets the "it's none of your business" treatment, as in this example of The Chairman of the Federal Reserve brashly avoiding congressional inquiry into loans of $553 billion dollars made by the Central Bank.

From Ben Bernanke's testimony on July 21, 2009 before the House Financial Services Committee:

The Silver Bomb

Representative Alan Grayson Democrat – Florida's 8th District asks Bernanke:

"What's that (the $553 billion)?"

Federal Reserve Chairman Ben Bernanke's Reply:

"Those are swaps that were done with foreign central banks..."

Grayson:

"So who got the money?"

Bernanke:

"Financial institutions in Europe and other countries..."

Grayson:

"Which ones?"

Bernanke:

"I don't know."

Grayson:

"Half a trillion dollars and you don't know who got the money?"

Bernanke:

"Um, um, the loans go to the central banks and they then put them out to their institutions..."

Grayson:

"Let's start with which central banks?"

Bernanke:

"Well there's 14 of them...I'm sure they're listed in here somewhere."

Grayson:

"Who actually made that decision to hand out half a trillion dollars?"

Bernanke:

"The FOMC Federal Open Market Committee."

Grayson:

"And under what legal authority?"

Bernanke:

"We have a long standing legal authority to do swaps with other central banks."

Grayson:

"Anything specific about it?"

Bernanke:

"My counsel says Section 14 of the Federal Reserve Act..."

An even more interesting exchange before Congress took place on leap day February 29, 2012 between the Fed boss Chairman Bernanke and Congressman Ron Paul as a ranking member of the House Finance committee. Congressman Ron Paul represents the 14th district of Texas. Congressman Paul, who also holds a medical degree, enjoys a national reputation as the champion of individual liberty.

He is known among both his colleagues in Congress and his constituents for his consistent record never voting for legislation unless the proposed measure is expressly authorized by the Constitution. Dr. Paul is the tireless advocate for limited constitutional government, low taxes, free markets, and a return to sound monetary policies based on commodity-backed currency. Paul's authorship of the "Audit the Fed" bill HR1207 is likely what precipitated the way he was introduced by house committee chairman Bachus who said to Bernanke,

"At this time Mr. Paul is recognized...your thorn in the flesh".

Congressman Paul took the microphone, and in a textbook example of understatement, agreed that he had "criticized the Fed on occasion". In an indictment of the complicity of Congress he added,

> *"but the Congress deserves some criticism too. The Federal reserve is a creature of Congress."*

In a political drawing of the saber Congressman Paul highlighted again the institutional secrecy and poor economic record of the Fed as he continued,

> *"and if we don't know what the Fed is doing, we have the authority and we certainly have the authority to pursue a lot more oversight which I would like to see. So although the Fed is on the receiving end, and I think rightly so, when you look at the record." Paul went on to address Bernanke again, "I mean The Fed's been around for 99 years almost a few years before you took it over...and 99percent...98percent of the dollar value is gone from the 1913 dollar. So that's not really a very good record."*
>
> *This is a graph of the official figures of the plummeting value of the dollar since the creation of the Fed.*

The Silver Bomb

Value of a $1 Federal Reserve Note in 1913 Dollars
(Source: US Bureau of Labor Statistics)

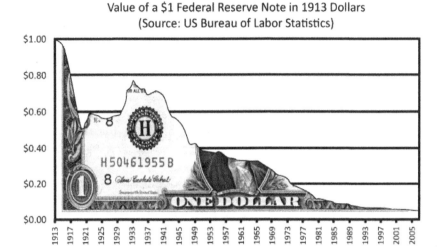

Congressman Paul explained the situation as he continued with this history making address,

> *"I think what we're witnessing today is the end stages of a grand experiment...a philosophic experiment on total fiat money. Yes they've been debasing currencies for hundreds, if not thousands of years and they always end badly. They always return to market-based money, which is commodity money -- gold and silver. But this experiment is something different than we've ever had before and it started in 1971, where we were actually given an opportunity in many ways to be the issuer of the fiat currency, and we had way too many benefits from that than people realize.*
>
> *But it's gone on for forty years and people keep arguing from the other side of this argument that it's working, it's doing well, and yet from my viewpoint and from the viewpoint of the free market economists that all it's doing is building a bigger and bigger bubble. And the free market economists are the ones who predicted the NASDAQ bubble... the housing bubbles, but we never hear from the Keynesian, liberal economists and the central bankers saying 'watch out, there's a bubble out*

there...there's too much credit...too many problems there...there's a housing bubble. We have to deal with it'.

Usually we get reassurance from the Fed...on that. But I believe there's a logical reason for this because the Federal Reserve is given responsibility to protect the value of the Dollar. That's what stable prices are all about. We don't even have a definition of a Dollar. You know, we ask about the definition of a Dollar, and it's "oh, well whatever it [will] buy.' Well, every single day it will buy less... the next day.

*To me it's like building an economy and having economic planning **like a builder that had a yardstick that changed its value every day**. Just think of the kind of building we would have. This is why we have this imbalance in our economic system. But it was a system designed to pyramid debt. We have a debt-based system. The more debt we have, and the more debt the Federal Reserve buys, the more currency they can print, and they monetize this debt. (emphasis added)*

No wonder we're in a debt crisis...it's worldwide. I think it's something we've never experienced before. And I think the conclusion will be a vindication either for sound money, or if you win the argument and say 'yes ...we are great managers...we know how to do it...we want the credit for the good times and we want the credit for getting us out of those good times.' I mean I think in a few years we're going to know. Of course I'm betting that the market is smarter...commodity money is smarter...nobody is smart enough to have central economic planning.

So I'm anxiously waiting for this day...for the conclusion, because reforms have to come. They are already talking about...when you see (World Bank head) Robert Zoellick talking about monetary reform, and talking about gold, our time has come for serious discussion on monetary reform."

After comments from Representative Barney Frank (D-NY) lauding Bernanke for the fine job he had been doing, Dr. Paul jumped right back in and asked Bernanke if he did his "own shopping at a grocery store".

Bernanke looked down at some offending dust-speck and fiddled with the boom of the microphone before answering that he did. Paul again laid into him,

> *"okay so you're aware of the prices. You know, this argument that the prices are going up about 2 percent, nobody believes it. You know, in the old CPI says prices are going up 9 percent so they believe this. Now people on fixed incomes...they are really hurting. The middle class is really hurting because their inflation rate is much higher than the government tries to tell them, and that's why they lose trust in government.*
>
> *But you know this whole idea about prices and debasement of currency...if you loan me a hundred Dollars and two years from now I gave you 90 back, you'd be pretty upset. But we pan back on that money and it's worth ten or fifteen percent less and nobody seems able to do anything about it. It's very upsetting. But it's theft if I don't give you your full $100 back, if you loaned me $100...somebody... I'm stealing $10 from you. Somebody's stealing wealth and this is very upsetting. But you know, last...in January at one of your press conferences you said that, uh...You sort of poked a little bit of fun at people, uh...to down play the 2 percent inflation rate. But if you say it's 2 and I say it's 9, let's compromise for the sake of argument and say it's 5 percent. Uh, you said it doesn't hurt you unless you're one of those people who sticks their money in the mattress. But, uh...where are you going to put it? Are you going to put it in a CD, and not make any money at all? So this...doesn't make any sense. It doesn't encourage savings, and it just discourages people.*
>
> *But I do want to make a point about prices. Prices go up. To me that is not the inflation. That is the bad consequences of the inflation which comes from the increase of the money supply and that's one of the bad effects. But you know, you took over the Fed in 2006. I have a silver ounce here. (Mr. Paul held up for view a 1*

ounce silver US Dollar), and this ounce of silver, back in 2006 would buy over four gallons of gasoline. Today...today it'll buy almost 11 gallons of gasoline. That's preservation of value, (Paul holds up the silver ounce again) and that's what the market has always said should be money.

Money comes into effect in a natural way. Not in an edict, not by fiat...by governments declaring it is money. But why is it that we can't consider, you know...the two of us, an option. You love paper money, I think money should be honest, Constitutional...still on the books...gold and silver legal tender why don't we use it. Why don't we allow currencies to run parallel. They do around the world. One of my options, you know, as much as I would like to do something with the Fed, I say the Fed's going to self destruct anyway when the money's gone. Why wouldn't we legalize competing currencies? Couldn't people save (holds up coin again)...put this in a mattress...get four, five times as much of the value in a few years?

So the record of what you've done in the last six years is to destroy the value of...money...of paper money. At the same time real money(holds up the silver eagle again) is preserved. But a competing currency... We already have a silver eagle. It's legal tender for a dollar. And some people say it's legal tender...it's a dollar...it's on the books, and they use it and they get into big trouble. The government comes and closes them down and they get arrested for that. But what would be wrong with talking about parallel currencies...competing currencies? This is something that Hayek talked about...something that I think would be a compromise and that we could work along those views."

Chairman Bernanke Replies:

"Uh, First of all...good to see you again, uh Congressman Paul (audible laughter breaks out to illustrate the irony). Um...just one word on the inflation. Of course those numbers are constructed by the Bureau of Labor and Statistics, not by the Fed. They are independently *constructed and I think they are done in a very serious and thoughtful way. Um, on alternative currencies...nobody prevents you from holding the silver or gold, or whatever you want to...it's perfectly legal to do that. And you're also happy to, uh...it's also perfectly fine to, um... hold other currencies... Euros or Yen or whatever else. So in that respect you can do that, and I'd be happy to talk to you about it."*

Representative Paul interjects:

"But Mr. Chairman, that is not money. I mean, when you pay taxes to buy a coin, or you have capital gains tax... If you have to settle a lawsuit...it's always settled in depreciating Federal Reserve Notes. It's never settled in the real contract. So that's nothing near money, uh...when it's illegal to use it. But to do it, you'd have to repeal the legal tender laws...you'd have to legalize this...you'd have to get over the sales taxes...get rid of the capital gains tax. In Mexico they are talking about this. They are trying to have competing currencies. They've been wiped out too many times with inflation. And it wipe[s] out the middle class. They are allowing people to start to save in a silver currency. So I hope we move along in that direction, because there shouldn't be any overwhelming changes all of a sudden that there could be a transition. People could vote on it. Maybe they would give up on a Federal Reserve Note and vote for real money."

Bernanke:

"I'd be very happy to talk to you about it."

Congressman Paul was *on the money* (pun intended). It **is** only a matter of time until we see the end of the Federal Reserve Note fiat currency. Bernanke knows it and so do those who are at the helm of the Regional Federal Reserve banks and all the while they are offering empty paper, they are loading up on metal.

As the populace increasingly sees how, as Mr. Paul put it, they have been "stolen" from, confidence in the banks could instantly vaporize and we see a cascade of fractional reserve deceptions failing at an accelerated pace, and their assets and debt collectibles coalesced under the skirts of the ever-bigger, biggest banks. They are not going down without a fight, and they are entrenched.

By manipulating rigged, cabal-owned markets and borrowing and bailing themselves out, the bankers will continue on a path which cuts out the public from profits, yet shoulders them with losses both visible as in taxation, and invisible as in currency devaluation.

The Fed deposits into "private bank accounts" (read: accounts that are held by **private banks**), which are deposits made with Fed created money (monetary base expansion), which of course the Fed charges the taxpayer interest for. Said deposits are held as currency devaluating cash balloons, which generate no GDP stimulus as they are not loaned out for the use of the public.

We don't have a free market based upon the exchange of goods and services for real money in the bank but instead, we have the debt creation machine of The Fed whose entire existence is based upon the creation of bigger and bigger debt. The National debt is held primarily in two arenas of either Public Debt or Intragovernmental Holdings. The US Treasury Direct website explains these as:

THE DEBT HELD BY THE PUBLIC IS ALL FEDERAL DEBT HELD BY INDIVIDUALS, CORPORATIONS, STATE OR LOCAL GOVERNMENTS, FOREIGN GOVERNMENTS, AND OTHER ENTITIES OUTSIDE THE UNITED STATES GOVERNMENT LESS FEDERAL FINANCING BANK SECURITIES. TYPES OF SECURITIES HELD BY THE PUBLIC INCLUDE, BUT ARE NOT LIMITED TO, TREASURY BILLS, NOTES, BONDS, TIPS, UNITED STATES SAVINGS BONDS, AND STATE AND LOCAL GOVERNMENT SERIES SECURITIES.

AND

INTRAGOVERNMENTAL HOLDINGS ARE GOVERNMENT ACCOUNT SERIES SECURITIES HELD BY GOVERNMENT TRUST FUNDS, REVOLVING FUNDS, AND SPECIAL FUNDS; AND FEDERAL FINANCING BANK SECURITIES. A SMALL AMOUNT OF MARKETABLE SECURITIES ARE HELD BY GOVERNMENT ACCOUNTS.

It is really a misnomer to call the resultant indebtedness of the private transactions of a secretive banking cabal "Public Debt". They are called public because the bond instruments created to pay for them are sold to anyone including the general public. If a member of the general public wishes to help pay down the debt without charging the government any interest on a mature debt bond, they can bypass the bond market altogether and make a payment either online or by mail directly into the coffers of the US Treasury. This is the recommendation on the TreasuryDirect.gov site:

YOU CAN MAKE A CONTRIBUTION ONLINE EITHER BY CREDIT CARD, CHECKING OR SAVINGS ACCOUNT AT PAY.GOV

YOU CAN WRITE A CHECK PAYABLE TO THE BUREAU OF THE PUBLIC DEBT, AND IN THE MEMO SECTION, NOTATE THAT IT'S A GIFT TO REDUCE THE DEBT HELD BY THE PUBLIC. MAIL YOUR CHECK TO:

ATTN DEPT G

BUREAU OF THE PUBLIC DEBT

P. O. BOX 2188

PARKERSBURG, WV 26106-2188

The US Treasury Direct website differentiates the Federal deficit from the National debt and explains how deficits have built up to the National Debt as:

THE DEFICIT IS THE FISCAL YEAR DIFFERENCE BETWEEN WHAT THE UNITED STATES GOVERNMENT (GOVERNMENT) TAKES IN FROM TAXES AND OTHER REVENUES, CALLED RECEIPTS, AND THE AMOUNT OF MONEY THE GOVERNMENT SPENDS, CALLED OUTLAYS. THE ITEMS INCLUDED IN THE DEFICIT ARE CONSIDERED EITHER ON-BUDGET OR OFF-BUDGET.

YOU CAN THINK OF THE TOTAL DEBT AS ACCUMULATED DEFICITS PLUS ACCUMULATED OFF-BUDGET SURPLUSES. THE ON-BUDGET DEFICITS REQUIRE THE U.S. TREASURY TO

BORROW MONEY TO RAISE CASH NEEDED TO KEEP THE GOVERNMENT OPERATING. WE BORROW THE MONEY BY SELLING SECURITIES LIKE TREASURY BILLS, NOTES, BONDS AND SAVINGS BONDS TO THE PUBLIC.

THE TREASURY SECURITIES ISSUED TO THE PUBLIC AND TO THE GOVERNMENT TRUST FUNDS (INTRAGOVERNMENTAL HOLDINGS) THEN BECOME PART OF THE TOTAL DEBT. FOR INFORMATION ABOUT THE DEFICIT, VISIT THE FINANCIAL MANAGEMENT SERVICE WEB SITE TO VIEW THE MONTHLY TREASURY STATEMENT OF RECEIPTS AND OUTLAYS OF THE UNITED STATES GOVERNMENT (MTS).

It is noteworthy that the word "We" is used above, since it is a very select group that decides how and when the money of the taxpaying public of the United States is spent. Not all of the National Debt is going to be paid. The Treasury website goes on to explain the difference between the Public Debt Outstanding (everything that is owed), and the Public Debt Subject to Limit (what is not actually slated to get paid, also referred as debt above the debt ceiling):

THE PUBLIC DEBT OUTSTANDING REPRESENTS THE FACE AMOUNT OR PRINCIPAL AMOUNT OF MARKETABLE AND NON-MARKETABLE SECURITIES CURRENTLY OUTSTANDING. THE PUBLIC DEBT SUBJECT TO LIMIT IS THE MAXIMUM AMOUNT OF MONEY THE GOVERNMENT IS ALLOWED TO BORROW WITHOUT RECEIVING ADDITIONAL AUTHORITY FROM CONGRESS. FURTHERMORE, THE PUBLIC DEBT SUBJECT TO LIMIT IS THE PUBLIC DEBT OUTSTANDING ADJUSTED FOR UNAMORTIZED DISCOUNT ON TREASURY BILLS AND ZERO COUPON TREASURY BONDS, MISCELLANEOUS DEBT (VERY OLD DEBT), DEBT HELD BY THE FEDERAL FINANCING BANK AND GUARANTEED DEBT.

It should be noticed that in the above website excerpt, "very old debt" is classed as "miscellaneous" and is deducted from the total Outstanding Public Debt. That's not a good sign if one is looking to the U.S. for long-term fiduciary trustworthiness.

Battles in Congress over the decision to raise the debt ceiling and authorize interest payment on ballooning debt which would otherwise be subject to limits, has been the central issue of recent "shut-downs" of the federal government. It is a phony fight staged for the mass audience over whether or not to allow the overweight debt creators to continue slopping at the trough.

The Silver Bomb

All the while the Fed is protected from scrutiny, while the image of the very nation it is exploiting gets tarnished. The world now sees in the United States a picture of a self-absorbed bully and of a squandering debtor nation which cannot pay its massive bills. Since the nation's entire budget now goes only to pay the interest on the massive sums of money already borrowed, it is unlikely it will ever catch up.

A world-altering change is coming, and for most Americans, it will be painful—especially for the unprepared.

Chapter 3

Papering over Paying the Piper
Monetizing the National Debt by rendering it insignificant through inflation
America can never pay back its debt.

Unimaginable trillions of dollars have been loaned into existence, created out of thin air to prop up the banks and the economy. America's national debt currently stands at 100% or more of GDP, with roughly half of that debt held by foreigners. The days of exporting debt are over, now it's time to default on it...one way or another.

Perhaps Vice-President Dick Cheney was right when he said that deficits don't matter. In a world where, at least for the moment, the debtor can literally print its own money, maybe it just really doesn't matter...or does it? The public, the corporate lap-dog media, even the complicit spenders in Washington all harrumph in agreement that the National Debt is a terrible burden to place on our children, or if not ours, then some future generation of children. In essence, they all agree that the debt is to be passed on to successor generations of children who will inherit the debt burden and grow up to shoulder their portion of the load as taxpayers.

Let this be the official formal invitation for everyone who still believes that the debt problem can be kicked further down the road to WAKE UP TO THE DEBT IMPLOSION AND FACE REALITY. The come-uppance is now, not upon future generations, but upon this one.

In the very near future, the severe consequences of building the American empire on a bubble of debt may end all discussion of anything but daily necessity. Those consequences are already past the point of just beginning to show. "The economy is in shambles," is a phrase often heard these days, but it is in reality far worse than that. If it were only that the economy was broken, it could be fixed. It might have been if America still *had* an economy. America's economy has been gone for a while. Globalization treaties and unfair regulation of domestic-based private enterprise have drawn the bulk of U.S. manufacturing away to more cost-effective off-shore locales. Much of the "smart money" has already left town, as many of those who see the handwriting on the wall and have had the wherewithal to do so have left the U.S., following opportunity elsewhere around the globe.

The U.S., as the world's largest market, is now primarily a consumer society which has been enabled to buy the world's goods and services based more and more on cheap Fed-driven consumer credit, and Fed-financed debit systems of outright dependency programs like Welfare, Food Stamps, and even Social Security. The sheer numbers of government-supported unfortunates who have already been devastated and forced to seek aid, such as the nearly 50 million households now receiving food stamps, is stark evidence that the financial collapse is fully in progress.

Precisely because the economy is on life-support, the Unemployment figures continue to soar. Without the sleight-of-hand parlor trick of just not counting the unemployed, the real unemployment figures are much higher than the "official" reports, with some estimates as high as 25%.

The bleak outlook for the U.S. economy has led some to quit trying to make anything happen for themselves and become the burden of others. Most egregious are the cases of "players" of the system, such as welfare baby-mamas, who see more children as a way to increase their monthly food stamps and government "paycheck," and fraudulent SSDI "mental" disability recipients, who in reality are often no more than substance dependant addicts or alcoholics who have learned that to claim mental illness is the fastest way to get a regular "disability" check. Walmart, for example, is full of stuff fresh off the fleets of freighters, primarily from China, that government-dole-dependant "Nut Check" recipients buy with their SSDI money on a monthly basis. Walmart stores are awash with government check moneyed shoppers around the first of every month.

There are many more signs that the crisis is well underway, such as in the still critically ill real estate market. Real estate values have continued to plummet despite "Fannie Mae" and "Freddie Mac," the bailed-out mortgage issuing branches of the government offering record low interest rates for fixed long-term mortgages. The greatest percentage of mortgages is supplied by these two government agencies.

In conjunction with commercial banks and aggregate mortgage lenders the government bundled these low-cost loans as investments and sold the "toxic" mortgage paper as complex securities to retirement hedge funds and investment managers. Millions of American savers, especially those who were expecting to retire on their mortgage-backed securities invested pensions got wiped out.

More home foreclosures are on the horizon as multitudes of buyers who found enticingly easy financing for homes, which they either never could, or can no longer afford, go underwater. No matter how cheaply they bought, millions of homeowners will be foreclosed on in the next few years. This cycle can clearly be seen to have begun with the crash of 2008.

Drastically falling real estate prices, combined with foreclosure-caused loss of property tax, and unemployment, underemployment, or financial calamity, leading to inability to pay property taxes, have all combined. The effect has been to strangle property tax base supported municipalities and cause county or even state governments to be stretched to the breaking point. State and Local government which receive from the federal government financial emergency funding will only be adding to the National debt

The Too Big To Fail Banks which created the entire debacle, spinning up new instruments of fractional lending fraud, all got bailed out to the tune of $16.1 trillion. That is, as long as they were playing for the team, which may not have been the case, for example, with un-bailed out Lehman Brothers which, it appears, was no longer invited to the party.

For those banks and companies around the world that were invited, the Fed printing presses went into overdrive. It obviously wasn't enough money though, because the need to repeat the process has been disclosed. At first it was what was just called Quantitative Easing or, simply QE. That was before it was fully revealed that subsequent rounds of QE would require enumeration to distinguish them. Now we have had QE 2 and what some have called QE "Lite", wherein the central bank theoretically reinvested the proceeds of its maturing holdings of mortgage-backed securities by pumping the funds into Treasury bonds, and all the while, we await the inevitable bonus round of money-printing of QE3.

QE3 has actually already begun, but it is not being called QE3. The January 2012 report from the Fed describes its goal to devalue the dollar by 33% over the next 20 years. Direct devaluation, even at a slow pace of 1.5% to 2% per year, has the same effect as flooding the monetary supply, and thereby inflating the currency. Added to this is the increasing clamor from banks for negative yield debt instruments, and for liquidity-providing Fixed Rate Notes. It has become a politics-as-usual shell game to hide the truth that there are only two options.

The first option is for the triumvirate of the Federal Reserve, the US Treasury, and the mega-banks to do nothing. If this course is followed, the liquidity crisis will continue to build to the point of revealing national insolvency. The central banks will systematically begin to fold *en masse*, at which point the world economy degenerates into a deflationary depression.

The second and only real option is to keep printing in one form or another all the way up to the point of hyper-inflationary boil-over. Again, this can take the form of actually printing the cash for Bernanke's helicopter-drop economy, or forced through devaluation of the Dollar, or in the creation of new Treasury products such as negative yield bonds which would force bond purchasers to actually have to pay in order to put their money into Treasury "securities."

While we have witnessed stunning denials from Fed Officials that sustained rounds of monetization would be implemented, we have the equally stunning demands from the banker controlled **Treasury Borrowing Advisory Committee of the Securities Industry and Financial Markets Association** (also known by some as the *Big Banking Super-committee That Runs The Whole World)*, which released a letter intended to direct the Secretary of the Treasury calling for the issuance of distracting, but nevertheless equally inflationary negative yield T-bills.

The cycle has been clearly demonstrated. When merely paying the interest, or the "service" of the debt, is more than the combined individual income tax revenues of all US taxpayers, and the size of the debt is beyond the liberal limits already allowed by law, then the presses are fired up again and more money is "created" to borrow from in order to pay off the interest on what has already been borrowed.

The bank cartel mouthpieces will again threaten financial ground zero if the debt ceiling is not raised…again. Lawmakers already afraid of getting plastered by the shut-down-the-government tar brush will gladly vote to hike the debt ceiling up to the stratosphere if need be…or even higher… if need be.

The U.S. Congress and the Federal Reserve along with all western central banks and governments appear to be un-deterred by the fact that a debt crisis cannot be solved with borrowing, bailouts and currency creation. Like trying to keep a home heated with only an open gasoline fire, the more you feed the flames, the bigger the risk of conflagration becomes. With only an "accelerant", which is useful only to get the real coals burning, but no long term plan for fuel, the risk is in burning down the house before anyone gets warm. The problem is not a liquidity crisis, the problem is a solvency crisis.

The next domino is the steady devaluation of the paper-backed paper through inflation invoked by the hyperbolic cash injections.

The net result is of course the clandestine default on the debt through debasement. Add to this the aggravating factors of announcements of plans for protracted currency devaluation, and the TBTF banker-demanded issuance of negative-yield Treasury debt instruments, and what results is the recipe for a hidden default accomplished with neither any visible fireworks nor audible pyrotechnical blast.

It could be like a lighter-than-air, noble gas-filled birthday balloon preserved for too long as a keepsake of a good time had by all. The balloon slowly sinks, until one day it is found to be drooping under its own weight, and following a painfully slow fizzle, finally losing its turgidity.

On the other hand, the default could yet be devastating, like the instantaneous destruction of a pin popping a balloon. This is especially true if it becomes evident that the Dollar is worth more dead, than alive. A series of runs against the Dollar by U.S. debt holders hoping to recoup at least part of their losses may trigger a slew of Credit Default Swap events, as the temptation may become irresistible to just burn down the house and collect the insurance.

The Silver Bomb

Myriad "experts" have made fear-placating and nervousness-abating statements touting economic recovery. Based upon cheery employment figures (which are really fictitious, manipulated figures), and the Housing Statistics (which do not represent unseasonal weather affects, or take into account the glut of un-bought, government owned REO or Real Estate Owned properties), and the deceptively un-eventful Euro-scene (if the fact that Athens is undergoing a "stealth" default is ignored), the pundits proclaim that the crisis was all just a harmless nightmare. They give soothing assurances that it is safe to go back to sleep and let the scary images fade into the memory hole. They coddle any doubts with firm guarantees about the "full faith and credit" that has it all backed up.

In absence of a catastrophic event, the monetization will continue and all debt may be technically repaid, and it will prove catastrophic for the US Dollar in its position as the world's reserve currency. All investors (foreign governments included) who have loaned to the U.S. will be paid off, but with Dollars that are so depreciated that being repaid is the financial equivalent of being on the receiving end of a Bronx cheer.

In the twisted world of intertwined economies and centralized international banking, what the lender calls debt is understood by the borrower as money. The default of a borrower creates a cascade effect as the loaned funds were likewise created through borrowing, until the default rises to the top of the debt pile where it is off-loaded onto the backs of the taxpayers. The central banks and the sphere of corporations that thrive around them enjoy private gain until it ultimately leads to public debt.

The monetary system, as we know it, is in the end stage of a terminal disease and its days are numbered. The great cascade default on impossible-to-repay national debts has already begun, and has triggered payment of credit default swaps as financially interdependent nations are unable even to service the interest payments of their sovereign debt. The increase of the respective money supplies by the western central banks will finally cease as a point of diminished returns is reached and no amount of added "loans" as denominated in the sputtering paper fiat currencies will be of any further value.

The game has changed. There are new players to contend with. The western empire is in the slow-motion process of losing control of the ball, and upcoming matches will be played on the other team's playing field.

The Silver Bomb

The End of Paper Wealth is Upon Us

Chapter 4

It Takes Inflation To Make A Bubble

Welcome to the World of Too-Big-To-Fail-Bailouts, Ballooning Sovereign Debt Bubbles, and the Big Bang Theory of Fiat Currency

The Debt Bubble had burst, and suddenly the US Taxpayer was going to have to pony-up and bail out the banks. The public was told that it was their fault for living so far beyond their means and buying things they could not afford. They were informed that it was poor performance by borrowers that had been the cause of the dilemma. They were told that it was going to be the-end-of-the-world-as-we-know-it scenario, if the financial institutions were not propped up, since they were so crucial to the economy, that they were *too big to fail.*

What convincing rhetoric that was. No one had heard the likes of it before. It sounded so grave and so important that it had to be true. In addition, what was being asked for was so enormous, that it really had the ring of actually being the conceivable size of the price tag to fix it all, when everything goes wrong at the same time.

That was just the first round. It was announced shortly thereafter that the situation was worse than had been suspected. It was broadcast how the delicate markets had been so hard hit that there had been a spillover effect in other sectors of the economy and how a feared crash of the U.S. economy was shaking the economic confidence of markets worldwide. In other words, the public was told that this was again about to become the financial apocalypse.

More banks needed rescue, both at home and abroad. It was not just banks that needed rescue, but businesses, and government, and the Federal Reserve System, known as "the lender of last resort," was just the entity to do it. There would of course be the usual exchange of securities plus the customary payment of interest as allowed by law.

Still that wasn't enough. The search for the guilty found no one in particular to pin the whole mess on. The discount mortgage underwriters and big banks, which being sure of governmental guarantee of insured deposits, made untold billions and billions of dollars in shaky loans and caused the whole solvency crisis in the first place, went un-prosecuted for fear of speeding up the pace of economic implosion. Even when convictions of wrongdoing were obtained against some of the most flagrant violators, the fines levied were infinitesimal compared to the profits made and were paid off as simply part of the cost of doing business. Giant financial corporations would simultaneously offer bundled investment products like Mortgage-Backed Securities, but would sell Credit Default Swaps which would pay off upon the default of the same paper and hedge their earnings by betting on both sides. Anything the big banks wanted to do seemed to be the new way of things.

The paralyzed, or in large part, uncomprehending U.S. public witnessed the nationalization of industry, including the takeover of General Motors, now disparagingly referred to as Government Motors. Contractual agreements between labor unions and management were abrogated in favor of government bailout and nationalization. American consumers were given the opportunity to turn in their old, already-paid-for family car and get a healthy rebate in the form of the "Cash for Clunkers" program, provided of course, that they helped to fuel the economy through purchase of a shiny new ride with special subprime financing for new vehicle buyers.

First-time home buyers were handed healthy Home Buyer Tax Credits as incentive to invest in a piece of the American Dream. The debt-strapped public was offered stimulus-package-backed ways to avoid foreclosure and modify upside-down mortgages, in the form of several rounds of government backed mortgage re-finance plans. Including but not restricted to programs such as, HAMP, HARP, Mortgage Write-down, Delayed Foreclosures, Government Support, "Operation Twist," Zero Interest Rate Policy (ZIRP), and even "Fraudclosure" settlements, the "recovery" has been built on the teetering stack of taxpayer-funded bailouts, tax credits and incentives. The final tallies of the debt shortfalls that all of these patch programs have attempted to treat are still not all in and may not be understood for years.

We now have the benefit of hindsight to be able to see the futility of all of these solutions that have been offered to boost the lagging economy. No amount of stimulus money or bail-out even begins to address the underlying cancer of debt. The crisis is a solvency crisis, and part of insolvency is not having the ready capital, or liquidity, to make purchases with. It has been ruffled-feather-`smoothing euphemism to refer to it as a liquidity crisis.

Taking the easy liquidity path of Quantitative Easing, the Federal Reserve is printing money like it's going out of style. That's because it is. The Fed is not alone, as the major economic powers of the world embodied as the eight largest central banks (the Federal Reserve, Bank of England, the ECB, Japan, China, Swiss National Bank, Banque de France, and Germany's Bundesbank) speed along together on the road to currency debasement as they all attempt to out-print each other. At the same time the central bank purchases of commodity gold and silver are accelerating unseen by the public eye.

The socialization of debts and privatization of profits can be attributed to the prevalence of government absorption of private financial industry losses, ease of borrowing from the Central Bank, and the lack of regulation limiting conflict of interest, like the cross-over between commercial and investment banking after the repeal of Glass-Steagall. The part lawmakers have to share in the blame cannot be understated, but may at least be understood since the most powerful lobbyists in Washington are in the financial sector, and have paid hundreds of millions to Congress and the Obama Administration.

In a Huffington Post article, Dan Froomkin writes,

"All this money makes Obama's top financial advisors veritable poster boys for the Wall Street culture that the president in his speeches has publicly decried as a "house of cards" and a "Ponzi scheme" in which "a relatively few do spectacularly well while the middle class loses ground...I'm not doubting the smarts of Obama's financial team -- but I do feel that the vast majority of people who take the kind of money we're talking about here can't help but be warped by it, and that in choosing to cash in, they essentially disqualified themselves from public service."

The Silver Bomb

Lobbyist money has long played a definitive role in the influence banks exert over legislation and have historically paid despicable sums to congressional financial committee members. There is a discernible tendency for favoritism in congress toward certain monopolistic corporations and sectors, particularly the financial sector. The most blatant collusion between government and private corporate interest is the special conditions enjoyed by the private central bank, the Federal Reserve System, as is evidenced by the Fed's fattened coffers. The recent increase in Federal Reserve assets will be welcomed by the shareholders who receive the statutorily mandated six percent in dividends.

The Fed, along with all of the western central banks, has enlarged its assets through debt making before, during, and since the onset of the debt crisis. The vast amount that has gone to bail-outs has helped balloon the National Debt to dizzying new heights with loans from the Fed. In a world of socialized losses, the debt been dumped on the taxpayers.

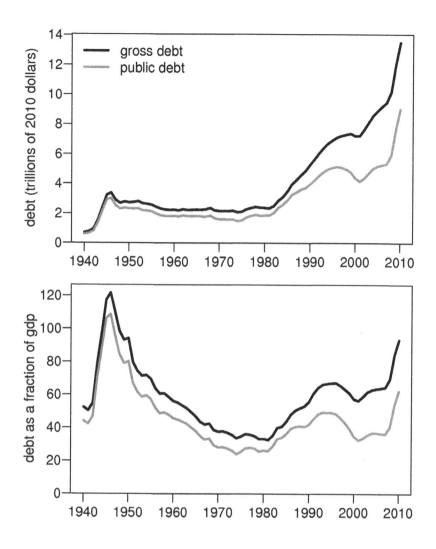

Desperate to maintain trade advantage, the central banks of the world are all locked in a death-race with the Fed as it rapidly approaches the brink of the abyss. It is as if while knowing that the present course cannot end up anywhere other than directly off of the cliff, none of them have a choice. To cut government spending and the subsequent ballooning of their respective national debts would gain the unwelcome attention of the masses who would suffer in the subsequent deflationary depression. Such high visibility would heave open for inspection the flagging curtain which is now barely veiling the mechanism whereby the central banks have exponentially increased their assets up to this point. Heads would roll, so that's not going to happen.

It is logical to assume that they have another plan. The first stage of the plan is to keep things the way they are as long as possible. There is still copious profit being made which must continue to be made as long as possible. There is also a reckoning to be avoided for as long as possible. It is entirely in the favor of the central banks and surrounding corporations to keep the truth under wraps as long as possible They are not showing any signs of flinching yet and are holding their course at full speed. Things are still working out well at the top and in what has become a global game of musical chairs, the central banks will continue on their present course until the last minute when the music stops and all players rush for the remaining seats provided by commodity money reserves.

Following a return to the commodity-backed currency, those who had been able to print unlimited "assets" in the free-for-all pure fiat money-fest world will return to the next best thing. They will seek to be able to dictate commodity money prices as they harness and control sufficient commodity money resources so that they can increase or decrease its supply as desired. The central banks operate as though they expect that they will always maintain their enshrined positions at the top of the financial food chain. They maintain the appearance that the crisis is over, that everything is fine, that they are in charge, and that it will always be so. The truth could not be more opposite. The aggregate truth is that the crises are not over; they are just beginning. Nothing is fine while private central banks are in control. The truth is that they only thought they were in control, and it's all in a state of change.

Like a technically defeated but not vanquished chess king that repeatedly escapes being in check by defiantly moving one more space and postponing the inevitable checkmate, the un-surrendered western empire is inevitably closer to being cornered. The game is almost over. The game is power and money. The power must go where the money goes...and the money is flowing east. The West has debt in the East. The bill is disproportionately large and getting larger and the payment of the bill is due. The debtor owes more than can be repaid even if everything was handed over to the creditor. The debtor has more of everything, uses more of everything, wants more of everything, and owes more than anyone. There is an imbalance.

Any imbalance will seek equilibrium. It may never actually be found, as perfect equilibrium is only possible in theory. A pendulum may never rest at perfect equilibrium as long as any force, no matter how imperceptibly small acts upon it, but it will always seek to do so. If imbalanced forces have temporarily overcome its tendency to center itself, and have held a pendulum to one side, it will never cease in its potential to swing to the other side. As soon as it escapes what is holding it, the pendulum must swing.

The Silver Bomb

The End of Paper Wealth is Upon Us

Chapter *5*

The Truth Managers
Social Engineering By Imperial Elitists Using The Mainstream Media They Own

Truthful information is the most valuable commodity on earth.

Like the proverbial element "Unobtainium", it is also the scarcest, most tightly-managed, and most costly to be without.

From the moment of our birth, we begin to process the information our senses are feeding us. We form our understandings of all aspects of life by what we perceive to be reliable information through our own observations and experiences, and what we are told or shown is true by those we trust, usually beginning with our parents. We continue to learn from ourselves, our family, our friends, and from those put in authority over us, particularly teachers. We continue to be influenced by role models, mentors, heroes (either real or legendary), and by exposure to what are referred to as the acceptable norms and conventional wisdom of society.

What we personally come to believe or "know" to be truth, is entirely subjective, as it is unfortunately dependent upon the accuracy of what we have perceived or been told. We can misperceive the information our senses are bringing us, either because we don't have the experience or basis of comparison to rightly process what we sense, or because of actual sensory defect. What we are sensing may have been altered, and worse, we can be lied to, most easily by some of those we think we can trust.

People look to the various media to find out what news is going on around them. The events of the day... at least as they are reported...are added to the conglomeration of perceptions that make up the current understanding of the news-seeker. The problem is that the main-stream media has long ago been captured by the global elite and is now an effective megaphone for the Empire. The media is the face of the empire and it is a primary tool in building and perpetuation of that empire. You may ask, "Why am I not hearing this on the news?"...maybe you should ask, "Why do they call it programming, anyway?"

The Silver Bomb

What is delivered in the place of factual reporting is a pre-packaged propaganda product designed to keep the masses quiet and directed and when expeditious, distracted and pre-occupied.

John Swinton was the editorial page editor of the New York Times from 1860-1870. When he addressed a group of journalists at the Twilight Club in New York City on April 12, 1883, he stated:

> *"The business of the journalists is to destroy the truth, to lie outright, to pervert, to vilify, to fawn at the feet of mammon, and to sell his country and his race for his daily bread. You know it and I know it, and what folly is this toasting an independent press? We are the tools and vassals of rich men behind the scenes. We are the jumping jacks, they pull the strings and we dance. Our talents, our possibilities and our lives are all the property of other men. We are intellectual prostitutes."*
>
> *"There is no such thing in America as an independent press, unless it is in the country towns. You know it and I know it. There is not one of you who dare to write his honest opinions, and if you did you know beforehand they would never appear in print. I am paid $150 a week for keeping my honest opinions out of the paper I am connected with. Others of you are paid similar salaries for doing similar things. If I should permit honest opinions to be printed in one issue of my paper, like Othello, before twenty-four hours, my occupation would be gone...We are intellectual prostitutes."*
>
> *--John Swinton, 1830-1901, Former chief-of-staff New York Times see The modern history project*

Multitudes who regularly witness discrepancies between media spin and real-life occurrence, are beginning to question the basic credibility of the managed main-stream media whose teleprompter-reader talking heads robotically repeat the sound-byte buzzwords and mantras they are given. This often results in them having a sudden realization that they have been living in a mainstream media generated illusion, which has been carefully crafted by adherents to the philosophies of Social Engineering and Central Planning. They begin to realize that there is no such thing as a free market, and that the first class of which to disappear was the free market of ideas.

> "The nation's immediate problem is that while the common man fights America's wars, the intellectual elite sets its agenda. Today, whether the West lives or dies is in the hands of its new power elite: those who set the terms of public debate, who manipulate the symbols, who decide whether nations or leaders will be depicted on 100 million television sets as 'good' or 'bad.' This power elite sets the limits of the possible for Presidents and Congress. It molds the impressions that move the nation, or that mire it."
> -- from "The Real War" (1980) by President Richard Nixon

The same power elite own the ever more monopolistic media. In 1950 there were 150 television networks. By 2009 there were 6 huge corporations that control almost all that is broadcast in the U.S. and they are in many ways, intertwined with each other. These corporations are vertically integrated and control every aspect of media generation from production through broadcasting.

Often referred to as the "big six" they are:

General Electric
2009 revenues: $157 billion

General Electric media-related holdings include a minority share in television networks NBC and Telemundo, Universal Pictures, Focus Features, 26 television stations in the United States and cable networks MSNBC, Bravo and the Sci Fi Channel. GE also owns 80 percent of NBC Universal. On January 18, 2011 the Federal Communications Commission approved Comcast's take-over of a majority share of NBC-Universal from General Electric. However, General Electric still has a 49% ownership stake in NBC-Universal.

Walt Disney
2009 revenues: $36.1 billion

The Walt Disney Company owns the ABC Television Network, cable networks including ESPN, the Disney Channel, SOAPnet, A&E and

Lifetime, 277 radio stations, music and book publishing companies, production companies Touchstone, Miramax and Walt Disney Pictures, Pixar Animation Studios, the cellular service Disney Mobile, and theme parks around the world.

News Corp.

2009 revenues: $30.4 billion

News Corporation's media holdings include: the Fox Broadcasting Company; television and cable networks such as Fox, Fox Business Channel, National Geographic and FX; print publications including the *Wall Street Journal*, the *New York Post* and *TV Guide*; the magazines *Barron's* and *SmartMoney*; book publisher HarperCollins; film production companies 20th Century Fox, Fox Searchlight Pictures and Blue Sky Studios; numerous websites including MarketWatch.com; and non-media holdings including the National Rugby League.

TimeWarner

2009 revenues: $25.8 billion

Time Warner is the largest media conglomerate in the world, with holdings including: CNN, the CW (a joint venture with CBS), HBO, Cinemax, Cartoon Network, TBS, TNT, America Online, MapQuest, Moviefone, Warner Bros. Pictures, Castle Rock and New Line Cinema, and more than 150 magazines including *Time*, *Sports Illustrated*, *Fortune*, *Marie Claire* and *People*.

Viacom

2009 revenues: $13.6 billion

Viacom holdings include: MTV, Nickelodeon/Nick-at-Nite, VH1, BET, Comedy Central, Paramount Pictures, Paramount Home Entertainment, Atom Entertainment, and music game developer Harmonix. Viacom 18 is a joint venture with the Indian media company Global Broadcast news.

CBS

2009 revenues: $13 billion

The New Empire is not limited to the United States, but is the global Financial/Military/Industrial/Pharmaceutical/ Corporate Plutocracy of today. It has grown beyond the original understandings of any single nation or kingdom. It is now a cohesive web of covert global affiliation, which extends beyond geography, race, religion, language, or any of the prior impediments to absolute hegemony.

> *"Some even believe we are part of a secret cabal working against the best interests of the United States, characterizing my family and me as 'internationalists' and of conspiring with others around the world to build a more integrated global political and economic structure - one world, if you will. If that's the charge, I stand guilty, and I am proud of it." -- David Rockefeller,* **MEMOIRS**, *Random House, New York, 2002, p. 405.*

The point of the greatest dominion of an empire is precisely the point of the beginning of its decline. This empire has grown to the point of having consumed all else and is now commencing to cannibalize itself.

We are in the midst of the decline of the American Empire

Whether or not it is publicized, we now observe a simmering, perpetual warfare to "spread democracy". It is not democracy that is being spread, but the continued dominion of the western empire. The false nature of that type of so-called democracy is starkly evident in the observable model of growing government tyranny over those living within the American Empire.

Seeking to be the world's only superpower, the elite-directed USA-led western empire spreads its controlled version of democracy with the use of "Shock and Awe" military prosecution In an Orwellian double-dose of double-speak, we are sold on the necessity of military "peace-keepers" to "maintain the values" of the International Community

And what are those values? They are the same as they ever were, in that wealth and power are pointed to as "Divine" endorsement of worthiness of privilege, or simply that rich equals divinely blessed. **The privileged ruling class actually see themselves as intrinsically more**

valuable than the rest of us. They see themselves as certainly more valuable than the "great unwashed" masses of "useless eaters", but also more valuable than the consumer class, whose wealth and liberty is extracted by the ruling class and are therefore seen as slightly higher on the food chain.

Human empire or monarchy is inherently evil. As a monarchy is perpetuated by the so-called "Divine Right of succession", so is the present Plutocracy perpetuated by exclusive insider-ism, and by nepotistic practices designed to "keep the money in the family". Wealth and the reins of power are presented from one generation to the next.

Within the life-span of any empire, there is always a revolving calliope of the same names and faces behind the scenes, which drive the policies of societal structure. As hind-site reveals, the nation-states of medieval monarchies were mere mirages of independent sovereignty. There was a behind-the-scenes coalescence of power, and merging of blood-line that the ruled masses were never privy to. There is within every ruling cabal an on-going power struggle for positioning at the top.

It is still the same today as the true ruling class members take turn at various positions of power like they were in a great game of musical chairs. Officers of the largest banks become Treasury Secretaries, or take their turn guarding the henhouse as chief council at the Securities and Exchange Commission. Revealing a behind-the-scenes continuity of power and influence over policy, the same insider names and faces appear from the term of one chief executive to the next. Carefully shopped from the ranks of the inner circles, or produced apparently out of nowhere with no discernible record of a past and announced with unprecedented media fanfare, Presidents are set up as puppet-head interfaces for the global elite, and democratically elected world leaders are ousted and replaced with "company men".

The present Western Empire dominates the entire world, and tromps under its feet, the residue of any non-compliant resistance. Black Ops intelligence networks are like the playthings of the elite, and are directed and funded by the secretive heads of the ruling Plutocracy.

Non-compliant Nations or any private entity are subdued through a broad spectrum of coercion methods ranging from economic pressure to military aggression.

The entire economic engine of the planet is propelled by aspirations of wealth to be derived through commerce with this juggernaut. It is almost a guarantee of game changing exposure for any well showcased product including probable national brand name recognition to secure nationally syndicated network affiliate advertising.

Any advertising attempt to drive a product's exposure through the media engine at the disposal of the world's most powerful is so expensive it effectively prohibits all but those with already deep pockets from affording it. This has the result of creating a wall of brand name product exclusivity and places a limit on who can get in. The whole world stands in shock and awe, wondering who can possibly compete with the money, the art and machinery of propaganda in movies and television, and the technological military superiority of this behemoth. Who can out-shout the ones who are holding the biggest megaphone?

The Silver Bomb

Chapter *6*

The Left/Right Paradigm and The Illusion Of Choice

Different Sides Of The Same Coin

Left versus Right. Liberal versus Conservative. Progressive versus adherent to existing precedent.

Polarizing viewpoints are continuously highlighted by the truth managing media. Partisanship is exploited to increase the conflict between the theoretically balancing halves of the total political landscape. The illusion of choice is maintained to appease the public yearning for a say in the way things are run and to give the appearance of some semblance of fair play. Contrary to the general thought paradigm, the will of the people, in real effective terms, it is quite moot.

As the election cycle heats up, millions of voters are focused on the candidates or platforms of the particular political party to which they have felt affiliation. Often they have followed the advice of family or friends in order to form their own individual political "leaning" with its basic platform or orientation. Others have been essentially handed their specific affiliation, as they were made to identify themselves with a media image produced to remind them of their own circumstances. Still others have attempted to make up their own mind by scouring the news for information that will help them make a choice. After careful deliberation, based on the information available to them, they may register to vote as a particular party member, believing they have sided with other like-minded individuals. They feel their vote will not be wasted if they add it to a larger collection of voices. They think they have picked sides.

There does exist a duality to government and to society, but it is not the simplistic and incendiary tribalism of left versus right, or one political party versus another. It is the less visible distinction of the tiny minority of chief executives, legislators, justices that are uncompromised in their duty to public service as elected representatives, plus what remains of the free press, primarily in alternative media, along with true free-market proponents all on the one side, versus the bought and-paid-for, over-arching machinery of the corrupt political system as orchestrated by the power-broker elite on the other. The control that the elite enjoy over the political, legal, and therefore economic landscape is in two major areas, these are in the influencing of elections and in the direct influencing of the decisions made by officials once they are in office.

This has the effect of rendering democracy, as practiced by the US and other developed countries, a shallow fraud. Few candidates today, most particularly for national elections, are in any remote way "the People's Choice" for who should run for office. Candidates are hand-picked by the moneyed elite, often very early in their careers. They may be tapped and slated for office even before they have demonstrated any aspirations for public service, such as while still in college or military service. Ambitious or ego-driven personalities are carefully shopped for the candidate mills of local party politics. Contribution money blurs the lines of ethics and idealism and the promise is made to them that they will go far if they voice support for their patrons. As a candidate shows potential to rise in the political hierarchy, they are plied with more money, favor, and countless other forms of largess designed to buy their loyalty. If they are given to indulgence, that will be enabled and encouraged as well, so as to provide a potential means of further control in the future through the threat of exposure of their scandalous excess. Any weakness in the candidate's character, be it greed or obsession, is a potential tool for coercive manipulation by the candidate's "handlers."

In our information overloaded world, electability of a candidate is more about positive widespread media exposure and opinion than anything else. Campaign advertising has become a grotesquely unfair arena where the more money that is applied the more exposure can be bought. This creates a built in lop-sidedness in favor of whichever candidate the money lines up behind. The electoral process in the United States has largely become mere theatre which is maintained, like so much else in the present climate, so as to not alarm the public and create a backlash.

By pretending that the voters, and by extension the ones they "elect", are in charge, the controlling insiders transcend political cycles in their multi-generational agendas to sap more money and power from their surroundings.

Money is used as a tool by those that have it to get what they want. It is no mystery that real international wealth carries the power to influence opinion and legislation, as it is so aptly said that, "money talks" and "he who has the gold makes the rules" From a profitability standpoint, influence that can be gained through the use of money is potentially a great investment. Over and again through history, we see examples of international money influencing the proceedings of ruling and legislative bodies inside government at any level. It is so pandemic that it is almost ignored as part of the normal scenery. In the time-honored method of using money to buy influence, the moneyed elite ingratiate themselves to targeted candidates with the blandishments that opulence can provide.

Occasionally, a particularly ugly example of bribery or influence peddling will surface that will get the attention of the public. When enough of a pattern is detected, in for example the effect of excessive campaign contributions, the calls for reform go forth. These become opportunities for the money powers to turn the game further in their favor. Such a ball in play can be fielded by the elite through the use of the officials they own and have selected and groomed for public office. Money-puppet lawmakers may appear to take up a populist cause on the surface, but are actually just co-opting the momentum of that cause. These same individuals will do the opposite of what they have led their constituency to believe they would do and actually sponsor legislation that will either neutralize any attempt at reform or insulate the interests of the back-room powers.

The elite's political puppets are expendable, and may be sacrificed on the altar of expedience in order, for example, to push unpopular but time-sensitive legislation. If the puppet lawmaker must be let fall to low opinion, it is worth it, if the background agenda can go forward. A popular political asset may enjoy a long tenure of consecutive terms which enables the gradual development of complex hidden agendas through the patient implementation of small but compounding steps.

Party affiliations are expendable as well. When the political climate within a party has become unprofitable or potentially hostile to the moneyed elite, they alternate to working through favorable members of the opposition party. Through the careful placement of controlled officials in either camp, their agendas go forward regardless of party affiliation. It is always the same agenda in place, and it is always the same group who are in power.

The actions of the imperialist ruler-ship, often contrary to the structure and laws of rightful governance, are laundered through layers of carefully selected, nurtured, and placed officials and lawmakers giving them the appearance of representing the will and authority of the populace. If there are any repercussions, it is often portrayed by the elite-owned media as having been the fault of the voters for not having thrown the bums out of office any sooner. Whenever it becomes necessary to cover the tracks of the elite, the media makes sure that the world understands that it was the people of the United States that dropped the bombs, or seized the oil field, or littered the economy with derivatives swindles. It matters not whether none of the American people actually had the chance to say anything about it.

The populace is slowly awakening to the fact that there is no real democracy at work. It is becoming less obscured that the real duality in politics and society is in the contrast between the moneyed elite versus everyone else.

Chapter 7

What Happens When the Great Correction Comes?

Which way will it go from here, and what you must do no matter what

Recession, Depression, Stagflation, Hyper-inflation...endless arguments abound about what lies around the corner. So, who's right? All of them are. **All of them are right...and wrong**. It may not even matter, since the future belongs to those who prepare. Fortunes have been lost, even in the best of times and fortunes have been made, even in the worst.

We are already in a **Recession** that will eventually prove to be far more devastating in scope than the so-called Great depression. Some of those who lived through the belt-all-the-way-tight times of the 1930's may take umbrage to that statement, but that umbrage could very well give way to a desperate search for daily bare necessities, especially for those who are unprepared. What we are going to see will unquestionably be the Greater depression.

Certain market areas may not be touched at all, but for the greatest majority, continued and worsening economic misery will be experienced. Part and parcel of the present recessionary, or let's face it, the present **depression** cycle will be prolonged corrective **deflation** in real estate values and in things we don't actually need to live. It is a buyer's market, especially in the luxuries market, for the foreseeable future.

On the other hand, for things we need to live, particularly, food, energy, health care, and even water, continued inflationary hikes in price will be the norm, followed, at first by sporadic, then increasingly frequent episodes of hyper-inflationary end-game price spiking. As hyper-inflation creates contractions in the economy, fear of deepening depression will continue to mount. For those who presently have the power to create money through the rearrangement of electrons, the temptation to do so will be too great. More "stimulus" money will be pumped into the system and more **inflation** will result. It will be a painfully slow war of attrition with the forces of overheat and hyper-inflation repeatedly battling economic anemia, and market malaise to a standstill The cost of living in real terms cannot help but continue to escalate, and the standard of living will decline.

The western industrialized nations have enjoyed global dominance and a higher quality of life than the world has ever known, and have done so for long enough that it is expected that it should always be so. It is so expected, that it is not even thought of as a higher quality of life, but instead is understood as the acceptable norm, or simply as the western *standard* of living. A rude awakening is imminent, particularly for millions of Americans who do not understand, or have not cared what is happening before their very eyes.

There is no mystery to the equation. The most basic fact of basic economics is that it is not long sustainable to spend more than comes in as income.   Also known as deficit spending, or living beyond one's means, this results in un-cleared debt and insolvency. By borrowing, in the form of the issuance of debt instruments that promise interest and by inflating the monetary base, in the form of currency printing, the central banks of the world have only postponed the inevitable. A great global financial reckoning is due.

A vicious cycle of un-sustainability has resulted wherein the assets of the privately held central bank are increased by charging interest to create debt for the Treasury in order to fund more spending, including for military aggression, in order to secure more resources, and to create larger profits for a select cabal of supra-national corporations, ultimately at the expense of the population. The collateral damage caused by following this policy cycle is assumed to be an acceptable cost of doing business, as long as it is not felt by those doing the damage. Like the ballooning cumulative budget deficits, aka the national debt, it can be ignored, as long as it isn't directly felt by those who owe.

The repeating of this cycle will most likely be the prominent feature of the decline of the Dollar which signals the last throes of the dying empire. It is unavoidable that those who now have control of the money mill will continue to use it, until they no longer can.

What is not avoidable is the inescapable end of the US Dollar dominated, empty paper fiat currency world. The temporary illusion of relief bought with more deficit spending through more money printing, or more accurately through more electronic currency expansion, will cease to be possible as the world will no longer buy the debt for sale in the form of negative yield US T-bills.

At the heart of the current monetary system is the level of trust extended to borrowers that they will repay what has been loaned to them. Complex systems of credit ratings, based on credit history, assets on hand, and future income are used to judge the credit worthiness of a borrower. It matters not whether the borrower is an individual looking to finance a house or car, a corporation wishing to use credit leverage for expansion or acquisition, or if it is a bank or even a sovereign nation in need of monetary liquidity. All are rated according to past performance, net worth, and present cash flows.

Trust is key in a debt–based economy. Only if lenders have a reasonable assurance of being kept whole through the borrower's loan repayment, with interest, can they afford to extend credit. Uncontrolled "stimulus" borrowing or debt creation by the central banks of the insolvent western empire has rendered all credit rating parameters as moot. As further loans are extended to un-worthy borrowers, especially to central banks and sovereign national treasuries, the entire concept of creditworthiness is negated. The rules no longer seem to apply, which calls into question whether they are actually rules. The more that the pattern of ignoring the rule book is rendered as the new *modus operandi*; the worse there is a lack of confidence in the overall debt system. When the confidence level wanes enough, a new crisis is faced. The result more and more is simply a **trust** crisis.

It has already begun. The Treasury is finding limited interest in T-bill auctions, as the realization is spreading that buying US debt instruments renders the buyer as just another player in a western-banker-officiated, and therefore rigged, game of global wealth consolidation. In December 2011, the Federal Reserve reported that holdings of U.S. Treasuries by foreign central banks fell by a record amount of $69 billion in the last four weeks of trading. Had it not been for increased purchases by the central bank of Japan, the drop would have been more pronounced.

The threat to the foreign holders of reserves of US Dollars and of US debt (the largest amount of which is held by China) is that should they attempt to get their money back and de-leverage out of the USD too quickly, the likely result will be an accelerated drop in the value of the remaining reserves of US Dollars that they still hold. There is significant potential for sparking off a large run on the Dollar, as other debt holders, as in creditors, see movements towards the door. This in turn could create a big enough drop in the USD's value that its holders may face outright default on the part of the U.S., and would be cut off from any hope of return on their investment.

China, and other nations, are quietly making their way to the exit from the United States home field with its fiat currency artificial turf of US Dollars.

Beginning with banks ramping up lending against physical assets of silver and gold, the intrinsic value of metal as money is again being recognized.

The Chinese government is actively encouraging their citizenry to buy as much silver and gold as they can. After decades of it being illegal for them to buy and own gold, The Chinese people are now doing so with great relish.

The economic powerhouses of the East, China and Japan, the second and third largest economies on the globe have begun bi-lateral trading directly from Yuan (Renminbi) to Yen and back again no longer using the Dollar as the medium of exchange and standard of evaluation.

China is already buying oil from Iran in gold, instead of in post Bretton Woods, post gold-backed (US) petro-dollars. Pressed by western trade sanctions, Iran is using gold bullion and oil as currency to pay for vital food supplies. Regardless of European Union sanctions against dealing gold in Iran, The Iranian populace is buying gold as a currency hedge against the uncertainty of their nation's future including currency depreciation.

These are but a few of the examples of the world-wide shift towards commodity precious metals as money.

There's simply no way out of this cycle until the dollar collapses, and is replaced as the world's reserve currency by silver and gold. The place where it became prudent to apply the brakes is barely visible in the rear-view mirror. The opportunity to let free market forces take care of deadwood economic underbrush, even if that translated to a bit of cleansing wildfire, was lost when the Too-Big-To-Fails where bailed out. The time for reform of securities definitions to end the creation of shameful confidence swindles such as toxic mortgage backed derivatives and default swaps has been postponed by the powerful printing presses over at the Fed. Lagging interest rates, which was coincidentally one of the conditions maintained during the great depression, are not going to be helped by the borrower-encouraging promise over at the Fed credit window to keep zero or even negative interest rates, creating a cap on the cost of money. The steps to prevent the present slide down this ever steeper and more slippery slope of currency debasement have already been blown past by the powers that be.

It is true already, but it will be more starkly evident in the near future. The truth is, if it is not in your hand, you don't actually own it. Bonds, stocks, even bank account balances are vulnerable to the slightest tremors of bank and stock market failure. As the people in Greece found out, it could happen in an instant that ATM cards cease to work and depositors cannot access their balances. There may be longer term repeats of times when stock brokers cannot buy or sell a single share for their anxious clients, since the markets have taken a holiday. When they do reopen, there is no guarantee that anyone's holdings will be fairly credited, or in the case of a total collapse, compensated for, or even if there will be any surviving record whatsoever that there ever were any assets.

It may not necessarily be a dramatic event at all. The potential exists for the collapse to happen in such slow motion that it will be imperceptible, not only to the average person, but to many avid market observers who will be distracted by watching closely for a dramatic occurrence, as the rug is incrementally, and therefore imperceptibly, pulled out from under them.

There does not need to be any actual interruption in daily business. It happened in the UK in the sixties, and recently in Switzerland. Depositors woke up one morning to find that the central bank had devalued the currency and any assets valued in that currency now had a fraction of the purchasing power that they had the day before.

The United States is the current location of the western imperial court, so it is incumbent upon the U.S. to attempt to shape the way things hit the bottom and how it all shakes out afterward.

The time in between now and the final reckoning will not be a pretty picture as the U.S. Government may resort to severe emergency economic powers as granted in the International Economic Emergency Powers Act (IEEPA). The IEEPA grants the President with the authority to act as an irrepressible dictator with the powers to seize assets, freeze accounts, and confiscate any natural resources deemed to be in the national interest.

It may be perceived to be in the national interest to confiscate all gold lying within the national borders. This would include the stored deposits of foreign holders of gold, if they are stored within the U.S., such as those held in the vaults at the Federal Reserve. As the greatest amount of physical gold is currently held inside the borders of the United States, doing so would position the U.S. to dictate the new global precious metal reserve standards, and shape the international currency again as it had in the past.

When the dust finally settles, a new U.S. currency, as well as all currencies that had formerly been tied to nothing but the US Dollar, will be re-issued in silver and gold, or at least will be some form of currency that is directly redeemable in silver or gold.

It may not necessarily be a U.S. currency at all. That may come as a shock to Americans, but it is not even a strange concept for people in many other countries. Those outside of the U.S. that up to the present have been used to trading in USD's are quite familiar with the concept. In the Philippines, for example it is difficult to find an establishment that will not take, and up to just recently, prefer to take US Dollars over Philippine Pesos. It may be a natural progression that transactions around the world, including even in the U.S., begin to be negotiated in a stable metal–backed currency. The shoe may soon be on the other foot.

The sheep led to slaughter who for whatever reason can't wake up to the truth, will see hard times. Those who position themselves to take advantage of the monumental trend we are now coming into will prosper. All cycles and trends have winners and losers. This is the grand-daddy of all trends in history and billions of people will not know what hit them but the few who took interest in the world that surrounds them and how it works and who prepared for the change will ride the wave of fortune. We will see mass wealth transferred from the paper/digital domain into the resource/tangible domain. Honest money is coming, are you prepared?

The Silver Bomb

The End of Paper Wealth is Upon Us

Chapter *8*
The *Silver* Bomb
The world's whitest metal is where the real fortunes will be made

Get ready for the Silver Bomb to go off.

We are on the brink of an absolute change in the economy of the entire world and particularly in the economy of the American-dominated western empire. For some, it is the brink of unfolding disaster, as none of the old ways will function and those caught in their mechanisms become the final victims. For others it is the brink of **unmatched opportunity** as we come face to face with a "cosmic alignment" of the forces of economy and history.

This moment will likely never happen again, and is destined to be the creation of some of the greatest fortunes ever imagined. These will be fortunes of substance, representing tangible wealth that is not tied to the whims of a controlling system of central banks. The history of man suggests that the coming moment (or what will be but a moment in relative terms) will be eventually swept away by another system, probably a truly global system, as opposed to the present western-dominated system. The time in between now and then will be the great reset of values of all commodities, across all economies that the world has ever seen. Items of intrinsic value will again have it attributed to them. Items that are in and of themselves worthless will return to evaluation as such.

As the value reset happens there will be no ignoring certain conditions that have never before occurred together and will combine to make silver to be the single greatest investment opportunity ever seen. This has never before happened. It is usually the opposite end of the cycle in effect as commodity metal is occasionally diminished in value. New discovery of vast amounts of a usually precious metal has occurred, which has negatively affected the price of that metal, such as the downward pressure put on Spanish silver and gold from the Americas.

For the few that understand the tremendous opportunity, silver is positioned for a price explosion. **The world is running out of silver.**

The Silver Bomb

It will be recorded when this phenomenon comes fully into view that the **Silver Bomb** has gone off, that it is over, and the silver is now essentially gone, except for the rare and accordingly-high-priced stashes of it that remain in private hands.

The world is consuming the metal silver like never before in all of history. Of all the silver ever mined which is around 50 billion ounces, only about 1 billion ounces, or 2% of it, still remains above ground, with the rest having been consumed as an industrial metal. Compare that to gold, which has been kept and not consumed like silver, so that of the 5 billion or so ounces of gold that has ever been mined, about 2 billion ounces, or *double the amount of silver* is still around. As a basis of comparison, the silver supply when measured in months of available silver has vanished so fast, that while there was 140 months of available above-ground silver in 1970, supply had diminished to only 50 months worth by 1990, and shockingly, there was only 11 months of available above ground silver to be had by 2010.

Most of the silver mined annually is consumed in all the electronic gadgets, batteries, windows, pesticides et cetera, in which silver is used, all of which after use, get thrown away. Once it has gone into these products, it is not recoverable. People worldwide are becoming surrounded by gadgets and gizmos that none of their predecessors had and proved they could live without. Today, their lives are so intertwined with electronic devices that they can't imagine living if they were suddenly deprived. The devices are all essentially disposable with short functional life-spans. They are delicate and get broken fairly easily, are not repairable by the average user, and are constantly in danger of becoming obsolete as they are rendered technologically out-dated by new versions or cutting–edge alternatives. The older models are essentially thrown away and replaced.

Of all metals silver is unique and therefore special in several ways. It is the most electrically conductive metal known. Silver is used in over 10,000 commercial applications, yet it does not get recycled because the arduous task of recycling only becomes cost effective if the price of silver is around $1,000 an ounce. Silver is being consumed at an increasing and alarming rate. It is alarming, in that it is being used up faster than it is being mined. It is believed that as much as 98% of the Earth's above ground supply of silver has already been consumed. The industrial demand for silver is approaching a half billion ounces per year which is over half of all silver produced annually. It continues to increase and is expected to possibly be as much as 85% of annual silver production by 2015.

In addition to the recent acceleration in its use, silver is not being extracted out of the ground as fast as it used to be. The annual amount being mined is less every year. There have been exceptional periods in history when huge, unprecedented finds of silver have recalibrated the basic value of the metal. Usually however there has been a steady flow of, if not "mother" lode-sized, then still sizeable new discoveries. These larger finds have historically added to the annual mining output. That is no longer the case. For the last decade, there have been no new discoveries of silver made that have been sizeable enough to affect the basic equation that silver demand has critically eclipsed silver supply.

Unlike Gold which is chemically inert, much of what makes silver so industrially versatile is the fact that it can chemically bond to other elements. The "tarnish" that is seen on silverware is a combination of the oxygen in the atmosphere with molecules of silver on the item's surface. Gold does not do that, and gold coins have been brought to the ocean's surface from the sight of centuries-old shipwrecks that looked as if they could have been minted quite recently.

Silver does occur naturally in its pure metallic "native silver" form, but it is exceedingly rare. It has been found more often in naturally occurring alloys with other metals, such as gold known as electrum, but still these are also rare.

The massive lode claims of the past were essentially concentrations of silver that were discovered in "veins" of a blue-colored material, which when assayed were found to be nearly pure sulphuret of silver. These massive silver-rich veins were, in places, hundreds of feet thick. These are essentially gone. Most of the silver being mined today is in the form of lower quality silver-bearing ores of variable concentration found in veins of only fractions of an inch. That is when it is found in "blue dirt" veins at all.

The Silver Bomb

Often, silver-bearing ore is discovered as the by-product of the extraction of some other, more concentrated metal. Base metal mines of, for example, copper, zinc, or lead have yielded silver from the left-over "tailings." The silver in most commercially-viable ores today does not come easily, as it is often "locked" in chemical compounds with other elements which must be separated in difficult and expensive chemical reaction processes. It may take the processing of incredible amounts of ore to obtain any recoverable amounts of silver. The Comstock Lode discovery yielded tons of nearly pure silver ore. Today, ore that yields a paltry 3 ounces of silver per ton is considered to be "high-grade". Existing silver ores are now the lowest quality ever seen.

There is no replacement for silver in its present role as an industrial precious metal. It has been used for centuries in the manufacture of mirrors, and more lately, in the manufacture of polarized and UV light-reflective glass, but that's not what is gobbling it up. It is, by comparison, silver's relatively new utility in the recently begun age of electronics which is proving to be the reason for its being consumed at such an auspicious rate. The societal changes brought about by the age of electronics have created a trend toward a high-technology hungry lifestyle that shows no sign of reversal. Silver is simply critical to the world of electrical and electronic technologies, and manufacturers and investors will pay whatever they must to own it.

Silver, as the world's greatest conductor of electricity, is used in electrical and electronic devices of every type. It is used in every television, telephone, computer and thousands of types of electrical contacts, switches, fuses, relays, and connectors. The exploding demand for silver is also being fueled by the voracious appetite for silver-zinc batteries which are common in small "personal" electronics such as watches, cameras and auto alarm remote control key-fobs. The recent spread of cell-phone technology in developing markets has demonstrated the demand for billions of silver-dependant, photovoltaic-equipped, solar-charged cell phones.

Silver has critical uses in the medical field as well. It has long been understood that silver has special antibiotic characteristics. The legions of the Roman army found that water would not stagnate if it was transported in silver urns. It remains the vessel and utensil metal of choice for the well off for a reason, as reflected in the old saw describing a wealthy heir having been born "with a silver spoon in their mouth." Surgical silver wire, screws, plate and staples have all found their place in modern surgical suites. Silver impregnated swabs have been used to sterilize the eyes of newborn infants and silver impregnated bandages are used, most notably, in the treatment of infection-prone burn victims.

It has been observed that molecular silver in a nano-particle form has effective general antibiotic tendencies. As is shared to a lesser degree in the case of zinc and other elements, silver is superior in its ability to thwart the reproductive cycle of single-celled micro-organisms, and it is believed, that of simpler mechanisms such as viruses. This growing field of research has found a loyal following in users of what is referred to as "colloidal" silver as a broad-spectrum antibiotic. Colloidal is a term that refers to the size of a particle being so small that it remains "in suspension"in a liquid such as distilled water. Colloidal silver is used to combat the growth of infection in external or "topical" application and in internal use, both when swallowed for targeting of digestive tract infection after which it must be followed by re-introduction of normal gut flora or "pro-biotic" therapy (silver targets all microorganisms and does not know the difference between good gut bugs and bad ones), and when used through sub-lingual absorption directly into the user's system.

At the same time that industrial use of silver is mushrooming, demand for silver as an *investment commodity* has blossomed to never before seen levels in the developing nations. Most notably, Chinese and Indian investors have taken to buying both gold and its cheaper running-mate silver as a store of their new found wealth. Investor demand is increasing along with industrial demand. This double demand has created a great part of the unique set of conditions that are now beginning to become apparent.

The supply of above ground silver, sought after for all of these uses, particularly in the last few decades since the advent of electronics, has been seriously diminished. The all-time greatest discoveries of silver have all but been consumed, returning the world's supply to scarcity levels not seen for over700 years. Demand for silver is high and silver supply is low. That is usually the recipe for sky-rocketing prices of any commodity. Usually it only takes motion, in either the supply or the demand of a commodity, for it to reflect in market pressure-triggered adjustments to price. Usually, if demand goes up, but supply remains constant, prices react to upward pressure and go up. Likewise, if demand is constant, but supply diminishes, prices also usually rise. Both of these changes reflect *more demand than can be met with existing supply*, and both are normally reflected in higher prices. If demand goes up at the same time that supplies diminish, the demand-outstripping–supply upward pressure effect is exponentially amplified and the price goes astronomically high.

Strangely, this has not been the case with silver...not yet.

Silver exists in the earth's crust at about sixteen times the amount of gold. That means that historically, there is about sixteen times the amount of silver being mined as there is gold. That has always priced silver at about one-sixteenth the price of gold.

There have been exceptions to the 16:1 rule, notably when the silver supply in the United States swelled with the discovery and development of anomalously rich silver finds, such as the legendary Comstock Lode. These finds of the late 19th century caused the issuance of millions of one ounce U.S. silver dollars, which were for decades the prominent form of common currency. The amount of silver flowing into the economy was a great factor powering the burgeoning national expansion of the United States of America.

Much of the wave of industrial mechanization of farming was financed with silver as the "silver farmers" as they were known were able to by-pass the central banks as they could receive low-cost silver money instead.

The effects of these forces began a running battle between the central banks who sought to control the price of silver, and free-market forces which would adjust its price naturally according to true supply and demand.

The manipulation of the silver market has been behind the scenes throughout the history of central banking in the U.S. including recently–surfacing evidence of banker collusion to manipulate silver. While market manipulation has been going on since there were markets, this practice has now gotten so out of hand that the news of it has leaked out into public view.

It began as part of the fallout from the 2008 debt crisis. Several banks took advantage of a competitor's illiquidity and absorbed them lock, stock and barrel, such as in March, 2008 when J.P. Morgan Chase (JPM) acquired the fatally-ill investment firm Bear Stearns. Part of what came in the purchase, were a massive number of Bear Stearns's existing short positions on silver futures contracts. A short position is essentially a bet that the price of a commodity will fall. Stearns's positions would be worth billions of dollars if the price of silver fell. It would have been a tidy sum for J.P. Morgan to have had bought ownership of. There was but one fly in this multi-billion dollar ointment and that was the rush of investors into silver positions as a safe haven for their hard-hit dollar-denominated portfolios. Were this to have had the normal effect, it would steadily drive the price of silver up. On March 16, 2008, the very day that Bear Stearns went out of business, silver had risen to a level not seen since the 1980's and hit the price of $21 per troy ounce.

This would have been devastating to J.P. Morgan Chase who was sitting on piles of bets that the price would go down, not up. Then the un-thinkable according to laws of economics happened. Inexplicably, from March 16, 2008 forward, when it was directly in J.P. Morgan Chase's favor, the price of silver fell nearly 17% lower. While the average investor scratched their head in disbelief and tried to fathom how this decline in the price of silver could happen, J.P. Morgan Chase was not only saved from catastrophic losses, but allegedly took on even more short positions and heavily increased their take.

Silver began to rebound and by July, 14 had righted itself to $19.30 per ounce. It again looked like JP Morgan was going to get clipped as they then held, along with the HSBC bank, at some estimates over 85% of the commercial net short positions in silver futures contracts on the COMEX. This would have allegedly caused them to have been in arrears for an eye-popping 169 million ounces of silver. Virtually equal to the entire COMEX warehouse stockpile, the second largest in the world, that much silver would have been roughly 20% of the entire world's annual mine production. There seemed to be no way out for JPM. Again, for no discernible reason, the price of silver began to sink...and sink...and sink even more, until it had lost over a third of its value in just thirty days, when by August 15, it stood at $12.82 per ounce. Then the bottom totally fell out and by October, silver was left gasping at a measly $9.00 an ounce. Many investors were destroyed, and for a moment, silver was so low it essentially could not be gotten rid of.

This was un-cannily fortunate for JP Morgan Chase who made an obscene amount of profit off of their gigantic, concentrated short positions. It is alleged that off of the drop in the price of silver from August 14 to the very next day of August 15, 2008, that JP Morgan Chase raked in $220,000,000. Considering that figure amounted to profits for just one day, the entire descent in the price of silver from March through October 2008 would produce incalculable profits for JP Morgan Chase and HSBC.

The metal commodities market is theoretically to be monitored by the Commodities Futures Trade Commission (CFTC) for illegal and unfair trading practices. They are expected to prevent unfair circumstances, such as not allowing a trader to corner a large enough concentration of short position holdings to be able to continuously hit the boards with a strong enough showing of short bids to be able to absorb any upward pressure and artificially cause a drop in prices, essentially manipulating the market. JP Morgan Chase's outrageous fortune finally caught their attention.

The story was run on March 9, 2010 by the New York Post that the CFTC in joint action with the Department of Justice (DoJ) Anti Trust division was conducting an investigation of JP Morgan's activities in the silver market. JP Morgan stated that they were not under investigation by the DoJ. The statement did not deny that JPM was under investigation by the CFTC. This would be followed by reports on the website of the Gold Anti-Trust Action committee (GATA) that a London-Based metals trader had blown the whistle on JPM and HSBC. The trader, named Andrew Maguire had apparently been aware of their on-

been accomplished for a margin requirement of only 10 percent of that. This allows the investor to cover more contracts, and carry more positions, as long as no margin call comes due which cannot be met.

Margin requirements can be changed to adapt to changes in investor or market conditions either by traders or altered or prohibited at any time by the metals exchange. The drop in silver between May 2 and May 6 2011 was simultaneous to a rapid-fire barrage of margin increases from the COMEX itself. In an increase of nearly 85%, the *initial* COMEX margin requirements (individual investors may be required by their broker or trader desk to pay more) were bumped up from $11,745 to $21,600. This is usually the time that margin requirements go down, or at least hold, as the drop in a commodity brings out lower futures prices, and usually lower margin requirements. It was not so this time, as margins were raised at the same time as the price was falling.

This pulled the legs out from under thousands of average investors who were forced to sell off their holdings to make the margin calls. The price was falling so their losses mounted as they got less and less for the assets they had been forced to sell. This motivation perpetuated more panic short selling and drove prices down even harder.

Eric Sprott, as one of the leading experts in precious metals markets carries a mantle of considerable credibility. Sprott is the CEO of Sprott Asset Management LP, a major league metal market player, wielding a hefty bat of $8.5 billion in assets under management. Not mincing words in any way, Sprott laid it on the line in the summer of 2011 in an interview with Silver Invest News, when he said,

> *"In my heart of hearts, I believe it was a manipulation...There was no market, it was a setup. They've just pushed it down. It's ridiculous...I think it was the short...the people who were short that were caught. They were losing gargantuan amounts of money and therefore, they initiated the attack on May 1."*

Likewise to King World News, Ben Davies, CEO of Hinde Capital explained in August of 2011,

The Silver Bomb

"Certainly along with many others in the market we understood the perhaps vile manipulation that was going on by some of the larger houses who, as we know, occupy that space... which is what we've been seeing..."

There are silver "smack-down" events that appear to be warning shots fired over the bow of voices in opposition to the status quo as well as social engineering events with the intended double–duty purposes of free market enthusiasm dampening and managed market-reflex conditioning.

During Congressman Ron Paul's historic "showing of the silver bullet to the fiat currency vampire" speech, as it has been dubbed, at the same moment when millions of Americans were looking right at Congressman Paul as he held a one ounce silver coin up in front of Fed Chairman Ben Shalom Bernanke, while describing the silver as being capable of "real preservation of value," the silver market was slapped down again by massive short selling and *it lost over 10% of its value in one hour.*

It couldn't have been said any clearer by the "banksters," as they are more and more frequently referred to, unless someone over at one of the big publicity firms had released an official statement saying,

"We're still in charge here...This is our market!"

That was the intended meaning of the manipulation event, and that was the meaning that everybody went away having an understanding of. At least they had some version of that understanding. Like motorists knowing that it could be punishable by the application of undue attention, which are careful not to make challenging and defiant eye-contact with the overly zealous officers at a choke-point traffic stop, many will deflect their eyes at such a moment, so as to not have to process the disturbing enormity of it all. Some who understand the idea that there is market manipulation happening, are thankful it is not them that got squeezed this time or that, and reckon events like this to be managed learning curve defining moments, where "The Powers That

Be" have given an instructive demonstration of the futility and expense of disobedient, independent, free market behavior.

At the same time that demand for silver is increasing at an alarming rate, the price is enigmatically low.

Metals are never bought as a producer stock. That is not their natural function. They naturally act as barometers of other factors in the equation. They are intrinsically valuable. That means that they represent a store of value in and of themselves. There is a certain level of effort and investment required to obtain them that is represented in their value. The rest of their inherent value is the utility they find in human endeavor and whether or not they are to be found as indispensible, which makes them wanted. Their value is inside their very molecular make-up which cannot be duplicated. They are, by cosmic design, the measure of the value of other things.

Regardless of how long it is that their intrinsic value is obscured or skewed, it will continuously reassert itself, and unavoidably make itself known. It is a factor of time. Things that have no other final destiny, other than that which is logically inevitable from current conditions, can be observed in their fulfillment of their destiny as predictably as the hands of a clock being expected to arrive at each hour on schedule.

Is there a collaborated effort to manipulate metals markets downward, so as to mask the lowered buying power of the now untrustworthy paper asset currencies of the western bankster empire? History will be the final arbiter, but soon the entire question will be quite academic.

With the opening of the Hong Kong Mercantile Exchange, silver buyers are not limited to the monopolistic, closed-loop markets of the west. The Chinese and all of Asia can now buy silver and take possession of it in Hong Kong. They can purchase from the Hong Kong "Merc" with Yuan directly from their bank accounts. They are not restricted to the minimum 5000 ounce contracts of the western exchanges. This will effectively allow for an end-run around the stranglehold of the western empire. Silver will be squeezed between high demand and low supply and the price will inevitably skyrocket.

The Silver Bomb

The End of Paper Wealth is Upon Us

Whistleblower Andrew Maguire put it this way,

> *"If just 1% of Agricultural Bank of China customers buy 500 ounces of silver, that would require 1.6 billion ounces of silver! I believe the leveraged and naked existing short side concentration in silver will be blind-sided by this. None of this potential new physical demand has been factored in by analysts and I expect a large and unanticipated drawdown of physical gold and silver over the next few months, ahead of the international contracts going 'live.' China is keen to diversify their cash holdings and is also encouraging citizens to make investments in gold and silver. The Pan Asia Gold Exchange is another step in this direction by opening up ease of access to physical gold and silver to their bank customers. This physical backed exchange is going to be a big game changer. This factor will ultimately destroy the remaining short positions in both gold and silver... In my opinion it will create a massive short squeeze."*

Rob McEwen a prominent gold entrepreneur has stated that for silver a reasonable price following a foreseeable increase in gold and using the 16:1 ratio, that *"$200 is conservative."*

Europacific Capital CEO Peter Schiff agreed in his statement,

> *"I think eventually silver north of $200 with gold over $5,000 makes a lot of sense."*

And Silver guru Eric Sprott, who has put his money where his mouth is by making a $1.5 billion bet on it, leaves no room for ambiguity when he says,

> *"It'll be the investment of this decade... it's only the beginning of things."*

The last run up in silver saw a 300% price jump from $16.00 to $48.00 per ounce. That will be nothing compared to the coming super-squeeze between east and west, when the dam finally breaks and silver takes its rightful place as a *truly* precious commodity metal.

The global silver market price will correct to potentially 10 times its present price, perhaps even more, and those who have positioned themselves in advance of that correction will see seemingly unbelievable gains from timely investments in silver.

The price in silver will not be kept down forever and when the actual demand for, rarity, necessity, and therefore value of silver can no longer be hidden and the truth emerges, the greatest windfall of the ages will be realized by those who have taken advantage of this special moment in history.

The Silver Bomb is about to explode.

The Silver Bomb

The End of Paper Wealth is Upon Us

Chapter *9*

Gold has nowhere to go but up
Before it's all over, gold will be $10,000 an ounce or higher

They have pulled the plug...the western elite central bank led cartel has...and it is definitely to their advantage to make it all hit bottom while there is still more gold in the west than in the east. The clock is ticking.

That advantage is changing day by day, and the developing giants of the east (China, India, etc.) may beat them to the punch. There is a new PAGE in the directory of exchanges.

The new exchange will be known as the Pan Asian Gold Exchange (PAGE), and it will be situate in the hub of eastern economic vigor. There will no longer be the need for global gold buyers to put up with the shenanigans of the London and COMEX exchanges, the U.S. government, or the Federal Reserve. The insider market manipulations of the western exchanges will not extend to the new market.

Many barriers presently experienced by smaller investors will be removed. Buyers will be able to take physical delivery of precious metal directly from the exchange. Lower contract limits will open the doors to smaller investors, and the commodity buying world will snap its attention to the east.

The western central bankers are quite aware that this is happening, but they are not going out in the flames of self-immolation that would be sparked off by announcing it publicly. They will continue on in their present course for as long as possible, which is being accompanied by a behind the scenes shift away from debt-based US dollar assets, and into physical commodity precious metals.

The routine will be for **all** of them to use their bloated asset stockpiles (real, as in the massive growth-fueled increases in the eastern monetary base, or imaginary, as in the Fed-distended example of western central bank created asset illusion) to load up on commodity metal. They will perform this routine as long as they are able to pass off their increasingly worthless fiat mirages called USDs, of which everyone is holding too much. The goal will be to try to enhance their possibility of performing a controlled crash-landing upon impact. The world has lost faith in the USD and all nations are quickly and quietly reducing their dollar-denominated holdings. It is all about globally exiting the dollar.

Once the loss of faith in any currency is widespread, it is on a one-way street to the dumping ground of history. There may be the occasional, and brief reprieve, or reversal of opinion, but like the chartable downward spike wounding of commodity metal prices caused by regular metal market manipulations which have not succeeded in a reversal of the overall trend upward, neither will momentary lapses of public or market memory reverse the fatal erosion of faith in paper (or electronic) currency.

Regardless of market manipulation, the price of commodity metal has managed not only to keep up with all other asset classes; it has provided a better return on investment than most. The price just keeps going up and the lower the level of trust in the paper (or electronic) US Dollar decays, the higher it will go. Detractors of gold as an investment have raised the specter of an imminent reversal in the rise of gold and silver prices, and have stated that the current price levels are an illusory projection of unfounded investor exuberance of expectation of metal price increase profitability. They say that the rising price is because gold is in a "bubble".

This is utterly ignorant or just plain disingenuous, as in reality, investors are flocking to precious metals, not as a profit-producer, but for the most part, as a value-holder. The resultant rising demand is rightfully reflected in the continued upward price direction. It is precisely that *there is a lack of confidence in other asset classes* that investors have sought the protective harbor of intrinsically valuable gold and silver. Gold is not in a bubble, trust is in a bubble.

The price of gold has repeatedly been found in a market-priced mode known as "backwardation" as basically the price of promised futures of gold is lower than the current spot delivery price. This is a normal effect of a shortage in the supply of a commodity when sellers with a deliverable quantity of the commodity can bid whatever the market will bear. Holders of such a commodity (which was likely gotten at below the current spot price) in such a climate can arbitrage or sell at the higher spot price and replace the asset again at the lower futures price and pocket the difference when the contract is settled. That is, if they have reasonable assurance that they can receive delivery on a future contract.

There is no reason that gold should be in backwardation, except for a lack of confidence that future contracts of gold will be receivable. It is much like the reaction of a commodity market to times of hoarding when there is plenty of a commodity, but none of it is for sale. In a backwardated futures market, a commodity price that is pledged at a future date may have been at or even above the spot price on the day it was offered, but by the time that the delivery date rolls around, the spot price is so high that the future price from before is now lower.

In a trade, the sellers offer is called the bid price and the buyers offer is called the ask price. Usually the ask hovers above the bid and it usually is a wash or even a loss to sell and re-buy the same asset. In a backwardated market pattern, where the spot bid price is above the futures ask price, buyers are displaying confidence in spot deliverables and doubt that the climate will improve, regardless of how comparatively attractive the futures price is made to be. Spot prices normally will only go so high, before they are too high, and the market will not bear it. Normally when the spot price goes high enough to extinguish the demand, the price corrects to a point that is closer to or below the futures price and the backwardation is eliminated.

This is not happening with gold because *the commodity that is in shortage is trust*. There is a shortage of trust in what is being offered in exchange for gold, which is the ailing paper Dollar. The trust shortage extends to paper-backed precious metals equities and ETFs. Buyers would rather have the physical product in hand than bet on a promise in the future. People do not, for the most part, buy gold as a speculative source of profit. It is true that apparent speculative gains (apparent, as these gains actually reflect diminution of the paper value, hence an apparent rise in price) could have been realized as the price of gold has marched upward, but that is not usually the reason why people buy gold. People also do not buy gold as a consumable commodity, which can be done without if the price goes too high. It is not a commodity that can be reproduced or replaced by anything else as suitable. It is not bought in reaction to waves of popularity, or to media attention either positive or otherwise. **People buy gold because it is good as money, and it will hold the value entrusted to it**. When enough confidence has been lost in paper currencies, gold cannot be priced high enough against it to stop the demand for it, and finally not high enough to encourage the selling of any more of it.

Observant traders have noticed the increase in volume of gold being bought by the world's central banks and many of the biggest corporations. All of the central banks had spent much of the past 3 decades diversifying out of gold reserves and into bonds, primarily US Treasury bonds. The flow has decidedly reversed, as the central banks are now diversifying out of paper equities and back into gold. As reported by the World Gold Council (WGC) the primary reason for the shift is,

> *"a continued desire among central banks to diversify their sizeable reserves in light of credit downgrades which have brought into question the safety of holding massive amounts of US dollar and euro denominated reserves."*

The WGC has reported that 2011 saw the purchase of 439 tons of gold by central banks, a level that has not been seen for close to fifty years. The net reversal of a gold selling to a gold buying trend began in 2009 and has increased. As central banks accumulate gold, there are already several countries that have suggested that their currencies be at least partly backed by gold, as in the case of the Swiss franc, or fully convertible and exchangeable for gold, as the Chinese have announced is the plan for the Yuan. In a departure from the London Metals Exchange and the COMEX in New York, the Chinese have offered the Renminbi Kilobar Gold, a gold spot contract denominated in Yuan as opposed to USDs. This is a fateful step toward the acceptance of the Yuan in the status of a gold-backed world reserve currency in anticipation of sounding the death knell of the US Dollar.

At the same time that central bank gold purchases have increased, the sales of gold from central bank reserves have essentially ended. Many central banks have begun to take steps to repatriate gold reserves they have had stored outside their borders in the vaults of other countries. Venezuela holds the largest percentage of its international reserves in gold of any Latin American country at over 60%. In 2011, in a move that was considered hostile to the west, but still made good business sense, Venezuelan President Hugo Chavez repatriated all of Venezuela's gold reserves that had been stored in European and North American banks. The bank of England, the oldest central bank in the world was obliged to cough up almost 100 tons of the yellow metal. Other banks in England, Switzerland, Canada, and one of the world's biggest metals trading banks, JP Morgan Chase in the United States were all hit up for the Venezuelan gold they held which amounted to a total of somewhere around 211 tons of gold being moved to vaults in Venezuela. Venezuela itself has seized vast oil reserves and infrastructure that lay within its own borders as it nationalized oil projects that were owned by U.S. energy producers. This resulted in a multi-billion dollar asset grab which is perhaps why Chavez may have feared a retributive seizure of Venezuelan gold reserves held within the U.S. Venezuela is now exporting that oil to developing countries, notably China. Chinese and Russian investors are putting money back into oil-loaded Venezuela.

The South American country is not the only example of national concern over the whereabouts of national gold reserves. Swiss Parliament is debating a measure called the Gold Initiative, that if passed would mandate an audit of and reveal the location of the gold reserves that remain of the property of the Swiss people. The German central bank is under increasing scrutiny as calls have gone forth for a full audit of Germany's gold holdings, including their storage locations. It is generally reported that the majority of the gold reserves owned by the Bundesbank, but held outside of Germany, are in the vaults of the Federal Reserve Bank of New York. Discussion of the question as to whether in the event of a currency debacle, there is likelihood of a U.S. confiscation of any gold within its reach has increased the anxiety over the German gold reserves being held in New York and other places outside of Germany. Concerns about the fitness of fiat paper currency to hold its value will continue to inspire holders of paper assets that represent inflation and debt to convert those paper assets to gold, and to seek physical deliverables instead of futures contracts. Concerns about the possibility of U.S. confiscation, will continue to inspire owners of gold held in the U.S. to remove that physical gold to beyond the confiscatory reach of the potentially dangerous flailing of a dying empire.

Following Venezuelan President Hugo Chavez, the central banks of the world are questioning whether to take physical possession of the gold they own, so that they may return it to safe-keeping within their own borders. This amounts to an official vote of no confidence in the promise that gold on loan or retainer, or that is simply being stored, will be returned to its rightful owners if a real currency meltdown were to occur.

It is particularly foreign–owned gold stores that are inside the USA that are feared to be the most imperiled. If the US Dollar crashes hard enough, the fear is that the U.S. will confiscate any gold within its borders, so as to have the leverage to influence the conditions for the inauguration of a (probably metal-backed) new world reserve currency.

Numerous large asset management firms have invested huge chunks of their clients' funds into precious metals for safe-keeping. These are examples of a general exodus into gold which are signaling wary traders that the time is coming closer to the end of opportunity to convert depreciating paper portfolio assets into gold.

Government debt is beyond any hope of amortization and the process of default has begun. The inflationary spiral is steadily and insidiously destroying the value of all US Dollar denominated assets. None of the fancy footwork or financial fixes that are advertised to treat the multitude of terminal financial illnesses has inspired any confidence in paper currency, in fact, quite the contrary. The bond market has already been given the cold shoulder as it has already failed to sell at the levels anticipated, triggering the Federal Reserve to buy up the surplus. When the auction fails to attract any bidders other than the Fed, the bond market will have become a ghost town were wealth would only go if it were looking for a place to die.

It goes without saying that the systematic accumulation of physical gold is the best way to profit during a surge in demand for gold. However, for the average investor, the window of opportunity to buy gold is closing fast. The time is fading to trade out of paper as the price of gold is already high enough to be prohibitive to many individual investors. When positions in the metal market are out of reach, there will still be action in the resource sector for a time, but that will come to an end as these markets begin to be denominated in metal-backed currencies.

Backwardation in gold futures is evidence of a market that is on fire and is consistently outpacing a normal futures price. It is also evidence that buyers essentially do not trust that gold future contract paper would be honored in gold, that the paper Dollar will hold its value as well as the gold, or that they can expect to be able to get gold in the future at any price.

When finally all faith in the futures market has evaporated in the heat of spot deliverables prices, there will be no more spot gold sellers of physical, deliverable metal. No amount of paper will coax it from hiding, and the paper currency will have collapsed. Gold will have effectively been removed from pricing against paper currency, and in the resultant split, the price of services and other tangibles will begin to be evaluated in gold. In very short order, the paper will be rendered meaningless regardless of its quantity.

At that point, no matter what happens, physical gold in hand will still have value. There is no other element on earth that has the unique characteristics of gold. Gold never changes as it is completely non-reactive, and chemically inert, so gold will be the same for every future tomorrow.

And for every tomorrow, gold will still be valuable...because it is gold.

The Silver Bomb

The End of Paper Wealth is Upon Us

Chapter *10*
Risk-Free Investing...Is It For Real?
What you need to know before investing in anything

Risk versus reward

This is the underlying fundamental dynamic behind every willful decision in life. Every time a choice in direction is made, it is a trade-off between the benefit to be gained and the potential for bad consequences. Disproportionate potential for a negative outcome of a decision can equate to a cost that exceeds whatever reward, or potential reward may have resulted. Alternatively, if the potential for gain is high enough, greater risk becomes more tolerable in trade. Most often, choices that offer the highest potential for reward are accompanied by correspondingly higher potential for risk. For some, any risk is too great and neutralizes any reward potential, for others it is just the opposite. Everyone has their own level of toleration of risk. Multitudes of influences, including background and present circumstances, combine within each individual to form their threshold of risk tolerance at any given time. It must be considered.

In practice, the only risks that can be considered are those that are perceptible in some way, be it from historical precedent, mathematical probability, discernible influence of known variables, or simply the laws of nature. The entire concept of insurance of every type is essentially intended to moderate risk. Making a "good" decision, where the reward mitigates the risk, boils down to possessing accurate information about all of these factors as it pertains to the decision. Since the goal of investing is to save and grow wealth, the risk factor is always an important element. A methodical investment plan can be undone by the losses resulting from unconsidered risk. Simplified, a diversified portfolio is often divided so that most of the funds are held in lower risk, even if lower potential yield, wealth preservation investments or assets and a smaller part of the funds are used as "risk-capital." These may be more freely "gambled" with in higher risk investments that have the potential to produce a positive return on investment and grow wealth.

It is primarily the first part...the wealth preservation part...the savings part of any portfolio that must be most carefully managed. Money is saved so it can be there when needed later, such as for realization of future plans, for retirement, or even provision for off-spring. Many investors and retirement savers were promised that their funds would be safe if they would trust in the security of blue-chip stocks, big-name brokerages and in various government assurances of full faith and credit, financial stability, and deposit insurance. Many investors and retirement savers have been obliterated in the aftermath of the dissipation of this investment security mythology.

Some retirement savers and investors were completely sheared as their Individual Retirement Accounts, which had been bundled in the hoppers of diversified mutual fund management firms and then sunk into high-risk "derivative" investments. They are derived from the bundling together of multiple debt instruments, such as mortgages, and sold as Mortgage-Backed Securities. They were given the highest credit ratings based upon the companies that offered them. The investors and retirement savers were assured by their brokers that these were the strongest and most secure places they could put their money. After all they were backed by mortgages, which are backed by real estate, so there was little or no risk and on top of that, they would see their money grow as the mutual fund realized a profit at the maturity of the "securities."

The problem was that these were not secure at all. They instead were toxic assets composed of upside-down mortgages, where due to the plummeting real estate prices, the properties no longer represented an asset that could cover the mortgage, and of "liar" loans where little or no down payment equity was taken in from unqualified borrowers to offset their inability to realistically swing their payments. The savers and investors believed they were making a safe move by opting for the sure and secure world of mutual funds. In reality, their portfolios were gambled on toxic junk. They were sold bad paper. They were told it was good, but it was bad. They were lied to.

The ones selling the paper knew it was bad and in the most despicable examples such as Goldman Sachs, made bets that it was bad paper. In the infamous *Abacus* Collateralized Debt Obligations (CDO) scandal, Goldman Sachs pushed through its brokers and affiliates the sale of risky CDOs, then bet short against them, through the purchase of Credit Default Swaps (CDS) which amount to credit insurance policies. If the insured security which had been bought with the hard-earned capital of the investors and savers were to tank, the credit default swap would pay off...big time. That is, it would pay off for the holders of the defaults swaps (read Goldman Sachs), not for the investors whose funds had just imploded. These are usually bought as a hedge against loss by the *owners* of the referenced debt-based security. They can also be bought by speculators who do not own any of the "investment" that is being covered from loss by the CDS and are essentially gambling that the referenced security will experience a "credit event" such as default. These CDS derivatives are usually offered by one company and are referenced to the offerings of other companies. In a legendary example of a total bankruptcy of ethics, marked by greed, corruption, and conflict of interest, Goldman Sachs bought credit default swaps on its own mortgage-backed securities or CDO products. The Credit Default Swaps would have made a mountain of money for Goldman Sachs. When charges were brought by the Securities and Exchange Commission, Goldman Sachs simply "settled out of court" without admitting any wrongdoing and paid $550 million in fines which were only a tiny fraction of what they had made on the deals. Except for the public relations black eye, it was very good business for Goldman Sachs. Meanwhile, the critical life savings of millions of American retirees were destroyed in a pit of corruption.

Others lost their assets when they were simply stolen by the brokerage house that they had entrusted them to. Corruption and cover up were the hallmarks of the MF Global Holdings scandal when the company allegedly raided customer accounts just before filing bankruptcy. It increasingly appears that instructions came right from the top as former Senator and Governor of New Jersey MF Global CEO Jon Corzine gave orders to use $200,000,000 (200 million dollars) of investor funds to pay off an overdraft fee owed to the London offices of JP Morgan. There are laws in the U.S. against the commingling, or mixing together of the funds of a brokerage house and those of its investors. In the international mega-corporate world that MF Global is used to, these quaint national law isolationistic trade barriers can be ignored by moving money around internationally. MF Global put the investment funds of its American clientele into accounts in London, where there are no such restrictions requiring the segregation of funds.

MF Global had overdrawn one of its accounts at the London Branch of JP Morgan, so they transferred the money from their customers' accounts to pay up. It was the combined money of investors, which did not belong to MF Global that JPM received. Cash-strapped MF Global had been up for sale to Interactive Brokers and had certainly wanted to keep up the appearance of being a salable, solvent, going concern. The "borrowed" funds probably would have been returned to customer accounts, had the deal gone through, but a few days before the sale, evidence of the missing customer "segregated" funds began to surface and the buy-out fell through. MF Global filed for bankruptcy Oct. 31, 2011. $1.6 billion in customer's funds are still believed to be missing, as if they had vanished into thin air.

The money had, of course, been stolen to pay off MF Global's gambling debts to the JPM grand casino-London Branch. Upon the dissolution of MF Global, the Bankruptcy trustee Judge Louis Freeh planned to use the amount of funds that could be recovered for MF Global's creditors (but not their customers) to determine the size of the massive "golden parachute" bonuses that its corporate executives would be paid. A letter bearing the names of 21 members of the Senate Agricultural Committee and calling the plan "offensive on its face" was sent to Judge Freeh pleading with him to not pay the bonuses. The letter points out that,

> *"It is difficult to understand why you would even consider paying anyone a bonus while nearly $1.6 billion in customer money is still missing. And it is absolutely outrageous to propose paying bonuses to the very people who were responsible for the firm's operational, legal, and financial management at the time customer money disappeared.*
> *A fundamental principle of commodities trading is that the firm's money must be accounted for separately and segregated from customer money. Throughout the long history of futures markets, no firm has ever lost*

customer money of this magnitude – until MF Global. The failure of senior management in this case is truly unprecedented."
--Letter to MF Global Holdings Bankruptcy Trustee Judge Louis Freeh from the Members of the Senate Agricultural Committee

Defunct MF Global has bilked thousands of its customers out of their money, and if the bankruptcy Trustee says so, the very perpetrators will be handsomely paid from the proceeds of the ensuing fire sale. The damage to the creditability of the entire commodities trading industry is indelible and is cited as the reason that many foreign investors now want nothing to do with U.S. equity and commodity trading houses. Even for the risk adverse investors who had trusted a major trader to wisely use and protect their money, this turned out to be the riskiest investment possible.

If preservation of value is the intended goal for a saver or investor then neither the bond market offerings of non-interest paying T-bills, nor the anemic interest rates of bank-offered Certificates of Deposit are anywhere close to keeping up with inflation. Even cash in hand is not safe, as the value of it is frittering away by the second through the hidden tax of inflation, as millions of dollars per minute are added to the money supply. When the inflation/deflation of the 2008-09 debt-based equities bubble burst, many saw how their carefully picked financial stocks could suddenly wither and die. All other equities classes including energy, real estate, the resources sector, and the short and long term bond markets and others all took unfathomable hits in value. Stocks are inherently risky. These are high-risk portfolio growth investments, not preservation of value investments.

Bank accounts, trade accounts, indeed all electronic accounts are as vulnerable as the power grid to innumerable forms of catastrophe, including the small but real possibility of Electro-Magnetic Pulse (EMP). Even NASA has warned of the real potential threat and is studying the sun's activity with the aim to be able to predict, or at least give some advance warning of Coronal Mass Ejection (CME) or solar flare events that may inflict damage to the electrical infrastructure due to EMP. Even human caused EMPs, resulting from a high altitude nuclear burst could potentially throw the affected areas back to a pre-electrified age. If such an event were to occur it would be years if not decades in *normal* circumstances to obtain the electrical replacement components, particularly transformers, to rebuild. With the exodus of heavy industry from the United States, none of these components are made in the U.S. The time it would take to rebuild the grid all depends upon the assumption that any manufacturing facilities are still in operation, and that if they are, that they are going to be willing to sell the parts needed to repair an EMP-disabled America. In line with the maxim that "If you can't touch it, then you don't really own it", money in an electronic account can disappear in a millisecond.

As the Dollar and all other fiat currencies have plummeted in value, it has reflected in the "rising" price of gold which has averaged nearly 20% per year gain against the Dollar for over a decade. The price of gold has not really gone anywhere; the value of the Dollar in gold has gone down. Real, physical gold and silver, in one's tangible possession, is the only guarantee against loss due to inflation, liability, failure of fiduciary responsibility, or downright criminal misappropriation. CDs, Mutual Funds, stocks, bonds, or paper cash, all of which are denominated in Dollars, cannot hold or preserve value in the long term. Only precious metal can do that.

Chapter *11*

Bullion versus Coins

There are definite advantages to buying the right kind of precious metals

<u>Disclaimer</u>: *this does not constitute, nor is the intent of the authors to give tax advice. Please consult your accountant.*

New precious metals investors may share a common misconception of what bullion is. The term 'bullion' simply means a refined and stamped weight of precious metal. Often what people think of as bullion is what is routinely seen in the movies such as *The Italian Job,* or *Three Kings*, or Ian Fleming's classic James Bond movie *Goldfinger*, namely big, heavy bricks of gold. In truth, bullion comes in many forms and weights, including bricks, bars, wafers, ingots, and coins. Gold bullion is then a recognized weight and fineness of gold that a person can buy for the current price of gold, plus the small percentage costs incurred in refining, fabricating, and shipping the bullion directly to them.

Bricks like the ones in the movies make up most of the world's gold bullion, which is owned by governments and central banks. These are the "London good delivery" gold bullion bricks of approximately 400 troy ounce size, refined and cast by the various private refiners worldwide, and accepted for 'delivery' into London and other major gold bullion markets.

The 400 troy ounce bricks are a cost-efficient way to buy physical gold if one has a working use for the gold such as in electronics, manufacturing, or the arts. However, if one doesn't make use of the gold, these heavy bricks can be costly to liquidate once removed from storage.

Holders of these may encounter assay, refining, or just handling fees in trying to liquidate that size of a gold bullion brick. It is much more difficult and time-consuming to liquidate gold bullion in a single chunk that is worth over $100,000, than it is to do so with the same amount of gold bullion in more convenient and tradable sizes.

The Silver Bomb

The small bars and ingots are often of exact weights and high purity and may be available in 1 to 10 ounce sizes.

The most popular form for household investors is in gold bullion coins such as the American Gold Eagle. Bullion is most commonly sought after in coin form by household investors. Gold coins are a practical and tradable form of gold bullion.

Alternatively, there are **semi-numismatic coins** that are not considered bullion such as the favorite $20 Liberty Head gold coin, which is still constitutional currency and far less likely to be confiscated during a dollar collapse than is bullion.

These old gold coins, like the Liberty Head Gold coins have a story to tell.

Beginning in the year 1849 and lasting until 1907, the American mint created gold **Liberty Head coin**s.

These coins were minted in several different denominations – two and half dollars, five dollars, ten dollars, and twenty dollars. All of the coins are made of 22k (90%) gold, with the twenty dollar editions containing nearly a full ounce (.96750 oz) of the precious metal.

Since all Liberty Head coins were minted well before 1933, they are considered to be non-reportable assets.

Buyers may not have to claim them as an asset or even fill out a 1099 for them, although they should always seek the advice of a tax specialist. Best of all, they are of an early enough mintage that the government cannot easily seize or confiscate them if a gold recall ever occurred again.

The Silver Bomb

Of all the available Liberty Head gold coins, the twenty dollar denomination is the true prize for investors. Since these coins contain nearly a full ounce (.96750 oz) of solid 22k (90%) gold, the gold coin prices are tied to the overall gold value on the marketplace. If the price of gold rises one hundred dollars, so does the value of these coins. Lower denominations of the coins contain less gold, but their value is still based largely on the overall price of gold on the market. Beyond the "melt" value of the raw material, Liberty Head coins have the added appeal of being collector's items. A limited number of all the different denominations exist, meaning that the demand for them is likely to increase although the supply never will. Originally the highest denomination minted was the Ten Dollar Gold Liberty. Due to the overflow of gold that began pouring into Philadelphia from the 1848 discovery of gold in California, Congress authorized the United States Mint to create a $20 gold coin on March 3, 1849. The $20 Liberty is known as the most popular and recognizable coin of its day.

The $20 Liberty, also referred to as a $20 Coronet, remained in production until 1907 when the United States Mint began releasing the $20 Saint-Gaudens.

Designed by James B. Longacre, the obverse of the $20 Liberty gold coin features a profile of Miss Liberty, sporting a crown which bears the inscription LIBERTY. Thirteen stars representing the original thirteen colonies and the date encircle her. The reverse features a bald eagle behind a striped shield. The words UNITED STATES OF AMERICA arc around the top of the coin. A total of three different types of $20 Liberties were minted during their time in circulation. Depending upon the date and type, other pieces of information are listed on the reverse, as listed below.

Type I: These coins do not feature the motto IN GOD WE TRUST and the denomination is written as Twenty D. Assistant engraver Anthony Pacquet created a second version of the reverse, but the redesigned coins were discarded and melted down.

Type II: The IN GOD WE TRUST motto was added to the reverse in 1866, resulting in the Type II design. Rev. M.R. Watkinson of Ridleyville, PA, spearheaded this change by asking Secretary of the Treasury Salmon

P. Chase to include the motto on the nation's coins in 1861. Such legislation eventually passed in 1865. Type II design change involved altering the shape of the shield on the reverse from straight to curved in the ornate rococo style of the day.

Type III: In 1877, the denomination was changed to read TWENTY DOLLARS instead of TWENTY D. This is the only difference between Type II and Type III $20 Liberty gold coins.

Another popular coin is the high-relief .96750 ounce gold piece coined between 1907and1933 and known by the name of its designer, the sculptor Augustus Saint-Gaudens, as the $20 **Saint-Gaudens double eagle**.

The condition of a coin, its scarcity and collectability, and more are not factors that come into play on the regular gold market. In short, coins will be worth more than their weight in gold due to their uniqueness. In some cases, certain coins can be worth <u>two or three times the value of raw gold in the marketplace</u>. Many investors have included several twenty dollar Liberty Head gold coins in their investment portfolio as a way of diversification and have enjoyed great returns on their investment as a result.

Many Americans are growing concerned over the United States economy and are looking for a way to protect their finances and wealth. Others want to find a simple, surefire, reliable, secure, and private method of investing their funds. Gold is certainly the answer. Buying gold coins minted prior to 1933 is the easiest, most affordable, most private, and most reliable way to invest in gold. Liberty Head gold coins are, in short, one of the best investments that can be made. Stocks and paper money may become worthless, but **gold is forever**.

Ironically, it is the 1933 gold confiscation that has made Pre-1933 gold and silver such a valuable asset to own. Many Americans are unaware of the fact that gold in the United States had been confiscated on three different occasions during the course of history. Gold seizures took place during the Revolutionary War as well as the Civil War, but, the most recent case of gold confiscation happened in 1933 during the tenure of American President Franklin D Roosevelt. A year later, in 1934, silver was also confiscated.

Franklin Delano Roosevelt issued a mandate through which all American citizens were ordered to forfeit all gold in their possession. The gold was turned over to the Federal Reserve and any citizen who failed to obey the order was subject to punishment ranging from substantial fine payment to imprisonment. The gold confiscation was not applied to jewelry and was extended to bullion and gold bullion coins only. The only exemption from seizure of coins made during that time were of coins of numismatic interest and those with numismatic value, which referred to coins with a minimum premium of 15% over the spot market price of gold at that time. The right of citizens to once again own gold was granted by the President on December 31, 1974.

Modern day American laws still grant the Federal Government the power to impound gold and silver when necessary (Read the recent **National Defense Resources Preparedness** executive order Obama signed into law). According to the laws put down in the 2nd chapter of title 12, of sub chapter IV, section 95A, the Feds can confiscate gold and silver, but under certain circumstances as stated,

"DURING THE TIME OF WAR, THE PRESIDENT MAY THROUGH ANY AGENCY THAT HE MAY DESIGNATE, LICENSE OR OTHERWISE—(A) INVESTIGATE, REGULATE, OR PROHIBIT, ANY TRANSACTIONS IN FOREIGN EXCHANGE, TRANSFERS OF CREDIT OR PAYMENTS BETWEEN, BY, THROUGH, OR TO ANY BANKING INSTITUTION, AND THE IMPORTING, EXPORTING, HOARDING, MELTING, OR EARNING OF GOLD OR SILVER COIN OR BULLION, CURRENCY OR SECURITIES".

Confiscating the gold and silver bars within a country creates an instant "bull" market as the global demand for the metal remains high while the supply available for trade is made even lower. The 1933 gold confiscation caused the price of gold to go up by 75% within the space of a few weeks.

Pre 1933 gold and silver "graded" coins have several advantages over modern bullion coins, the first of which is in the area of **privacy**. The graded pre-1933 gold and silver coins are the last of the few investments that can be acquired privately and kept confidential. Certified U.S. gold coins have been graded and guaranteed by the **Numismatic Guaranty Corporation** (or **NGC**) and **Professional Coin Grading Service** (or **PCGS**).

These numismatic gold and silver coins are completely private and investing in them can be done without letting even a single person know anything about the transaction. Paper investments made through banks and brokerages require them to make a full disclosure of your investment to governmental agencies. In many cases, this information is sold to marketers. However, this sort of intrusion into your private transactions is completely absent if you invest in pre 1933 coins. They do not even require 1099B form to be filed when you buy or sell your holdings.

__Disclaimer__: this does not constitute, nor is the intent of the authors to give tax advice. Please consult your accountant.

The Silver Bomb

A second and highly significant advantage of numismatics and semi-numismatics is their historically **good investment performance.** According to the CU 3000 Index numismatic coin performance standards, a $1,000 investment of generic gold coins bought in 1970 was given a current value of $22,500. A coin portfolio of mint state gold worth $1,000 during that same time period was found to now be worth $57,977. Compared to the Dow where the $1,000 worth of investment made in 1970 grew up to $13,500, the difference is huge. The U.S. has experienced fifteen recessions since 1919, but regardless of how the economy fared, the value of numismatic rare coins has consistently performed well. During the horrific stock crash of 1987, for example, the CU 3000 Rare Coin index went up 660%.

Confiscation concerns: The executive order passed by President Franklin Roosevelt on April 5, 1933 stated that it was illegal to own bullion gold bars or coins. The exact terms of the order stated that under the order of the President, all citizens were required to surrender all gold bullion coins, bars and certificates to the Federal Reserve Bank by the 1st of May, 1933. The hoarding of gold bullion, certificates, and coins was forbidden. The exceptions were those gold coins which had some special value as rare or unusual coins. Anyone violating the terms of the mandate was fined an amount of $10,000- an unbelievably huge sum in those times- or they were imprisoned for ten years, or made to suffer both. Even any officer, director or agent found to be a participant in another's act of violation was not spared and also punished.

If history is at all useful as a guide, and it is, then gold and silver will most likely be confiscated once again in order to back a collapsed dollar. Nothing is for certain, but it is certainly logical. Will the government confiscate pre-1933 metal? Perhaps, but at least the easier and more likely preliminary confiscation of bullion would be a warning to take action. There are, however, many reasons why pre-1933 coins are apt to again be exempt from confiscation

A case for PRIVATE gold & Silver pre-1933 coins: Will gold & silver bullion be confiscated?

"An interesting piece of information that you might not know is that the old U.S. gold coins minted prior to 1934 are still, according to the US Constitution, the only legal tender in our country. That is why there is such a strong argument about those coins being exempt from a future confiscation."
--Kal Gronvall, Gold & Silver Exchange president

Under the U.S. legislative laws, bullion can be confiscated upon orders from the President. Coins of rare and numismatic value, however, do not fall under the category of bullion and are considered collectibles. In comparison to the bullion market, Pre-1933 Gold is a small market. It is the needle in the hay-stack, where bullion bars and coins are the hay-stack that can be taken with an executive order. In the world of collectible or "numismatic" coins, each coin class, year, mint, and grade would have to be evaluated by the Government in order to set a buyback price. The man-power and resources to do this are great, and for this reason alone, the cost would outweigh the benefits. Bullion, which makes up roughly 95% of the grab-able gold, is easy to value and therefore cost-effective to seize. Considering that the pre-1933 market is a small fraction of the size of the bullion market, it is unlikely that government would waste the time and resources to go after this niche market.

Pre-1933 Gold coins are presently the safe haven of safe havens, the buying and selling of which is private, and requires no 1099 reporting, and in addition, they are unlikely to be confiscated. This makes private pre-33 gold coins a better investment option than bullion.

That opinion is by no means unanimous and there are those who present several arguments to support their disagreement. The sites and blogs which disregard the facts that support the pre-33 coin freedom from confiscation issue are often biased in favor of their own bullion products, and therefore have their own marketing agenda. Usually, a bullion-only dealer that persists in spreading the rumor that pre-1933 gold coins can be confiscated at any time has an easily understood ulterior motive. Pre-1933 gold coins are the biggest competitors for bullion dealers thus causing bullion dealers to lose out on business. That is a major reason why bullion dealers try to convince buyers that pre-33 coins can be confiscated just as easily as bullion coins or bars.

In the event that any site or person is found to be proclaiming that pre-1933 coins can easily be confiscated, their reasons must be carefully examined. It may be that they are curably ignorant or have been misled by a third party, but it also may be that they are deliberately feeding their customers wrong information. Upon examination of their financial motives, it will soon be clear whether they have another agenda.

The debate about numismatic collectibles in general is not nearly as vigorous as the particular debate about pre-1933 United States coins. Quite a controversy has arisen which points to deeper issues about legal money because pre 1933 coins were minted by the U.S. Treasury in accordance with constitutional law and thus are considered to this very day as the only constitutional currency. The Federal Reserve Notes in circulation as U.S. Dollars are creations of the Fed and hence are un-constitutional.

The coins which are used for common everyday transaction are of course legal tender. Dimes, quarters, dollar coins and half dollars are commonly accepted units of currency. But there is another interesting bit of information related to legal tender money. Any gold coin, minted by the U.S. Treasury before 1933, can also be considered as legal money, which is the actual reason why pre-1933 coins cannot be confiscated. The government can confiscate gold, but they cannot seize public money.

In 1933 when President Franklin Delano Roosevelt ordered citizens to turn in gold and silver bullion, he gave them printed money in return, but even after paper money had become the more accepted mode of payment, these pre-1933 coins have their same monetary value. Their status as constitutionally minted legal tender has not changed. In the United States, they are still considered as valid money even though they are not used at face value in commerce and trade.

When investing in precious metals, most people immediately think of gold as their best option. But silver has been used as currency for just as long, and minted coins made of silver can be traced back thousands of years. It is certainly a bit more affordable than gold can be, but can provide the same stability and investment returns that its more famous precious metal cousin does. In the final analysis, when at long last it is evaluated fairly, investment in silver will completely eclipse investment in any other asset including gold as the inevitable result of **The Silver Bomb**.

In America, one of the single most important silver coins ever minted is the **Morgan Silver** Dollar. Coming into circulation in 1878, this coin has become more popular than almost any other coin on the market. Commemorative edition coins and even the famous twenty dollar gold piece are still not as popular as the Morgan Silver.

Made from ninety percent silver, all of the original Morgan Silver Dollars were issued prior to 1933, allowing them to be considered a non-declarable asset. In addition to not having to file a 1099 or any other form of report with the government, the infamous 1933 act ordering confiscation of gold and silver did not apply to these coins. In short, no matter what happens to the U.S. economy, investors will be able to take solace in the knowledge that this investment will remain in their hands and remain valuable. The Morgan Dollar is one of the most collected silver coins in our history. Created to absorb the massive quantity of silver minted from the Comstock Lode the Morgan Dollar was designed by George T. Morgan in 1878.

The head of Lady Liberty takes up most of the obverse of this silver coin. She is encircled by the date of issue, thirteen stars, and the words, E PLURIBUS UNUM. This phrase, which translates to "Out of Many, One", was first chosen for official United States use in 1776.

The reverse features a bald eagle with wings spread perched upon a branch and arrows. The eagle is partially surrounded by a wreath. Above his head sits the motto In God We Trust. Around the rim are the words UNITED STATES OF AMERICA separated by a star on either side from ONE DOLLAR.

Morgan, who studied under the direction of instructors from the Royal Mint in London, placed an "M" on both sides of the coin to lay his claim to the design.

The largest and heaviest silver coin since the Civil War, the Morgan silver dollar contains a hefty 0.77344 ounces of pure silver. It was minted continuously from 1878 to 1904 when the government exhausted its supply of silver bullion. Congress would pass the Pittman Act in 1918, recalling over 270 million silver dollars for melting and the Morgan dollar would be minted one last year in 1921 before being replaced by the Peace Silver Dollar.

There are a number of factors that determine the worth of Morgan Silver Dollars. The current market price of silver directly affects the value of Morgan Silver Dollars, since they are made almost entirely of the precious metal. As the price of silver rises, so will the value of these coins. Conversely, the basic price of silver is not affected by many of the factors that can drive up the price of Morgan Silver Dollars. These are collector's items, after all, and their value can increase due to a coin's condition or the current demand in the collector's market for it. Add to that the fact that these coins are in a limited supply, and the Morgan Silver Dollar values are historically much greater than the basic price of silver.

Millions of these coins were minted to help absorb the massive amounts of silver found in the Comstock Lode in the late 1800s, but in 1918, over 270 million silver dollars were melted down to help provide relief to Great Britain during the First World War. Obviously, this increased the scarcity of the Morgan Silver Dollar and added to its value. Over the years, there have been numerous newer issues of the Morgan Silver Dollar for sale. From basic mint runs in the Sixties to the occasional commemorative edition, none are nearly as valuable or sought after as the original, early Morgan Silver Dollars.

Gold will certainly never lose its appeal, but neither will silver. For many, the affordability of silver makes it a more attractive investment option. There is certainly no denying that anyone can benefit from investing in these precious metals. Far and away the easiest and most reliable method of purchasing silver is to buy reliably graded Morgan Silver Dollars. Their value will continue to swell throughout the coming economic crisis, helping whoever owns them to rest a bit easier at night. The *Morgan Silver Dollar* is a great way to position one's portfolio to take advantage of the soon manifestation of **The Silver Bomb**.

One of the rarest coins is the much sought-after 1921-22 Silver **Peace Dollar**. These were the only years that this coin was minted in high relief. The Peace Dollars were minted between 1921 and 1929 to commemorate the signing of the peace treaty between the U.S. and Germany at the end of World War One, which was known at the time simply as *the* World War. It was believed that no other war could be worse than this one had been, and this was to have been "The War to End All Wars.

Interestingly this silver coin was created without a new Congressional Act instead it was minted under the provisions of the Pittman Act which had called in and melted down most of the Morgan Dollars. The medalist Anthony De Francisci designed the Peace Silver Dollar using his wife Teresa as a model for the personified head of Liberty. Above her head appears the word LIBERTY and beneath sits the date of issue. The motto IN GOD WE TRUST appears around her neck separated between the words WE and TRUST.

The reverse of the coin features a perched eagle on a mountain crag looking off into rays of sunlight. Across the eagle is the dollar denomination. The Mint Mark appears underneath the word ONE. At the top of the coin along the rim lay the words UNITED STATES OF AMERICA above the Latin phrase E PLURIBUS UNUM.

All Peace Silver Dollars were struck in high relief in 1921, their first year of production. The design was slightly modified in 1922 and normal relief coins were struck later that year. Peace Dollars were struck continuously until the effects of the Great Depression were felt in 1929. The U.S. Mint began producing the Peace Dollar again in 1934, but coins dated 1935 would be the last to see circulation.

Coins of this type from all nations are just as rare. If all the semi-numismatic coins of not just the U.S. but of the world were to be distributed throughout USA, only about one in twenty five people would end up owning such a coin. From that perspective alone, it puts these coins in the "exceptional" and "rare" categories and therefore not subject to confiscation. Arguments to the contrary are grossly inaccurate. The dealers that spread fear to the contrary have obviously taken a lot of liberty with the truth in order to endorse their own bullion products.

Buy gold and silver, especially silver. Buy it now. Consider the privacy, security and risk-abating exemption to confiscation of pre-1933 collectible gold and silver coins, especially silver. Buy as much as you can, for there will never come an event like the coming global return to metal as money in combination with the inescapable re-evaluation of all assets against the new value of precious metals, particularly the new value of silver. Then and only then will you be ready for **The Silver Bomb**.

Chapter *12*
Pace Yourself
You're in this for the long haul

Timing is everything.

It is usually in hindsight, looking back after the fact at some event or other, that it can be clearly seen that *when* a decision is made or action is taken was as important as *what* that decision or action is in the first place. Life is an endless string of cause and effect, and the timing of each and every decision made along the way determines the outcome as much as any other factor. Decisions can be premature, or they can be too late. It is only by taking into account the facts in evidence at any time that any success at timing can be seen.

Understanding the nature of timing, and making decisions and taking actions at the most optimal time is often a matter of discipline. Decisions that are based upon attainment of immediate reward such as the short-sighted seeking of instant gratification can resonate further than intended. There can be repercussions that extend far beyond the benefit of the short-sighted goal. In 1387 Chaucer wrote the CANTERBURY TALES in which he included the truism that "In wikked haste is not profit." This was re-worded by John Ray in his 1678 A COLLECTION OF ENGLISH PROVERBS as: "*Haste makes waste*, and waste makes want, and want makes strife between the goodman and his wife." In simplest terms, by seeking premature gain, one may end up losing more than was sought after in the first place.

It is the practiced discipline of putting off the natural tendency to seek instant gratification that enables one to plan out, commit to, and achieve long-term goals. The delaying of gratification will often free up resources that allow for the implementation and realization of longer term plans. This longer term approach includes the potential for the ultimate creation of actual conditions that provide for on-going enjoyment of the very same type of gratification that was delayed.

A simple picture of this is the dilemma of choice faced by the hungry farmer at planting time. Does he eat the seed in his possession, in which case he is momentarily satiated, or does he plant the seed so as to be able to produce a crop, reap a harvest, have another year of food to eat and realize a profit of having seed to plant with again the following season. Of course there are endless variables that will affect the outcome of this little example, but they do not affect the basic principle that if the crop seed is eaten out of hand, no possibility exists for future enjoyment.

The other side of the timing issue is to react too slowly to information or to disregard the facts in evidence until it is too late and miss the optimum moment. It is said "He who hesitates is lost." History tell us that 80% of investors will not get excited enough about an opportunity in time to profit from the particular trend and end up buying when things are at the top and selling as they hit the low.

Some are frozen in their tracks when faced with a decision and suffer from the "analysis paralysis" of looking too long before they leap. This is especially disabling in the world of intra-day trading when opportunity for reaction to miniscule changes can only be taken advantage of by the timely and skillful execution of judicious actions of the technical trader. This is not that kind of microcosmic investment opportunity. This moment in history, which will see the manifestation of **The Silver Bomb**, is the sum total of all the years, of all the days, and of all the trades ever made. It is more like becoming aware of the seeping cracks appearing in the face of a dam just before it bursts, or hearing the muffled grunts emitted deep within a mountaintop snowpack just before an avalanche.

The entire premise of this book is that the world, particularly the western world, stands at the edge of the change of an epoch. As it has been pointed out in these pages, much of that change will be repetition of cycles that have been observable throughout human history. *It will also include events that have no prior precedent and will never happen again.* The decline of the western empire, with the concurrent paradigm shift away from the fiat currency based economy resembles past historical precedent. It is understandable as a discernibly cyclic phenomenon, the pieces and parts of which can be seen in prior empires and prior ages. The collapse of an experiment with paper currency followed by the re-monetization of precious metal is also nothing new. The change that is coming that has never been seen before will be due to the global realization of the new intrinsic value of silver due to the never before seen consumption of it as an industrial metal.

It is the combined timing of this new rarity of available silver on planet Earth, with the unfolding events of the west-to-east transference of wealth, and the unfolding global return to metal as money that have set up the soon to be witnessed triggering of what has been referred to in this book as **The Silver Bomb**. The price of silver is low...right now. It is about to go up at a rate that can and will only happen once in history. The release of this book, or others like it that address the same topic, may have an effect in the further acceleration of the paradigm shift towards awareness about the new rarity and therefore the new relative built-in value of silver. That has been a great portion of the drive to deliver this information into the hands of as many as possible, and as quickly as possible, even though doing so could actually shorten the time-frame of the present window of opportunity to take advantage of the simple, practical recommendations herein.

Now is the time. It is the time of all times to go long on precious metals and particularly to go long on silver. It is time to buy physical precious metal and actually hold it in your possession. It is time to put every resource that can reasonably be used into silver. History tells us there will be price fluctuation and as we have seen, ALL markets are currently rigged and subject to wild volatility due to massive manipulation. These manipulated fluctuations are all based on the exertions of a central banking cartel whose goal is to hide the truth and perpetuate the paper dollar fraud as long as possible. The game has changed however, with the global economic shift to the east, and that western banker cartel influence will soon end. Pay no attention to price volatility in the interim. The change, that is described in these pages as **The Silver Bomb** will be unmistakably different from any of the present or even historical price fluctuations. If you buy silver one day and the next it drops 20%, don't let this shake you because that 20% loss is measured off of the current illusion of wealth; the US Dollar, which again, with all other currencies and assets that are denominated in dollars, is going to crash. It is at that point that those with physical metal, especially *silver* in hand are going to be the new RICH of the new era. Don't look back in other words. Buy it with both fists now and don't look back.

Chapter *13*
Storage
Now you own it...Where should you keep it

In the present western industrialized society, there is a complex system of distribution that brings the everyday things of life to most people. There is little need and less interest in storing all the things that are instantaneously available. There is a sense of ease and inattention to where things come from, borne in the understanding that whatever is wanted is obtainable by just taking a short trip in the car to the local store. But what if suddenly all of that were no longer to be the case? More and more evidence points to that scenario soon being a very real and vivid reality for most Americans.

It has been said that "people don't plan to fail, they fail to plan." It is precisely the "What if?" parts of life that are the hardest to plan for, but some basic ground rules can be followed. A few simple realizations are helpful in basic "contingency" planning.

First, one must realize that many, if not most of the murmuring multitude simply will not hear the clarion call to action. It is built into the gene pool perhaps, but it always seems to be so. There is simply no way that everyone will become aware of the condition of things. Others will ignore whatever uncomfortable information does not neatly plug into the puppet show picture and distorted data that the truth managers have provided them. Although the build-up to the present state of emergency and imminent event horizon has actually been long reported and loudly broadcast, not by the managed main stream media, but by other, more trustworthy sources, that it is only the heavy dosages and industrial strength of the numbing narcotics of big network news that has deafened them.

Like the mob that may perish in a burning theater, when they finally do understand their peril enough to be alarmed, it is often too late. The panicked crowd is trapped by the sheer number of them that have suddenly plugged the exit in an attempt to escape. The increasing smell of smoke had been ignored as irrelevant while the make-believe movie still played. Not until the flames reach the projector or the big screen itself melts down and the horrified crowd reflexively yells "FIRE," will they believe they are in danger, as they are trampled or trample others in a rush for the door.

Even when the general understanding is that action must be taken, like when the captain of a cruise ship announces that the reason the vessel has been listing so hard, is that it has been taking on water and is sinking. The captain calmly directs all passengers to begin to make their way to the lifeboats, but in the ensuing panic, orderliness and civility are soon thrown overboard. Precious moments are lost in spontaneous battles for possession of whatever looks buoyant, and many will be locked in the mob as it presses for the last of the lifeboats. When the struggling throngs find themselves in the water, they may begin to drown each other in an attempt to remain afloat, and will swamp any lifeboat within reach, overwhelming it in an attempt to survive.

The *zeitgeist* is beseeching all of humanity to question the current paradigm and to take steps towards preparation for survival of and prospering in the coming shift. Sensing the already unfolding catastrophe inherent in the collapse of cabal-controlled collectivism, a certain number of individualists, and seekers of truth have begun to systematically store supplies of every possible kind. Lambasted in the main-stream media as "kooks," these characteristically self-reliant and sensible "preppers", as they are known, are quietly stocking up. It is unfortunately a small percentage of the populace that is doing any of this...so far.

That only a few have awakened is, ironically enough, to the distinct advantage of the "early adopter" of the practice of saving for the rainy days ahead. The stampede has not started yet, and only part of the herd has begun to move. The mavericks that were comfortable outside the drove in the first place have run off already, their now distant hoof-beats having actually gotten the attention of some of the ones already in motion. There is still plenty of *stuff* to be had...for now.

There is another shady slice of society who may see what's coming but choose to rely on the preparations made by others, which they will beg, borrow, or steal in the moment of crisis. These are the ones who didn't just "fail to plan," as it is their "plan to fail to plan" all along. It is these, and those they can conscript into their service who will be, or potentially will be users of brute force in order to take whatever they want or think they need. This may include the commandeering of supplies by predatory, rogue government as has been provided for in dubiously legal decrees from the powers that be.

Whatever store of value that is visible and accessible to this crowd is potentially to be forfeited by the one who stored it. The most basic rule of security is therefore that stockpiles must, by necessity, be saved in secret. It would be nice to be able to share details with everyone, but due to the danger of foul play by the shady slice sector above either in troubled times or quieter times, that is a fantasy at best.

If an item or stockpile of items is too large or otherwise inconvenient to hide, it must be camouflaged. It can be hidden in plain site by appearing to be nothing of interest. It can be utilized in a stand-by role, or disguised as something common or useless. The innumerable examples in nature of flora and fauna blending in with their environment can forever be drawn from for ideas.

Keeping a prudent reserve of any useful thing is never a bad idea, if space permits. Perhaps one's choices in what types of property or facilities are under one's control should take the potential for wise storage into consideration. Not everything needs to be given the same level of discrete security. Whether someone sees a stash of toilet paper, for example, is not as important as how safely and secretly out of sight the investment silver is. A hidden safe is a very good idea.

There is no end to the possibilities in security storage designs and installations but regardless of what is implemented, it must be kept secret from all but the most trusted of one's associates, including family. Just because someone is family, does not mean they should ever be entrusted with information that could potentially result in loss, if they are not of the caliber to be known as reliably trustworthy. General tendencies of people should be considered in the light of possibility of facing a very different set of stresses and temptations. Someone, who in quiet times is essentially "cash register" honest but has other personality traits, which if amplified are potentially a liability, hazard, or security threat, may not be a good candidate to take into one's confidence. Care must therefore be exercised in the choice of with whom one shares any vital or sensitive information, including about what is stored, how it is stored, and where it is stored. None of that should be casually discussed as each topic may give away another.

It is best to just maintain as low a profile as possible before, during, and after the hard reset on the horizon. This is just plain common sense. The few moments where true heroism is called for most often happen in unseen anonymity anyway, so there is no advantage to undue fanfare. In times of trouble, as far as possible, it is simply best to be able to keep one's goods out of sight and out of mind.

Like every significant event in history, the details of the coming transition will be different for every individual. Specific changes in circumstances will require flexibility and adaptability. It may become necessary to quickly switch to other plans, as different decisions are made to duck and cover, break and run, stand and fight, or batten down the hatches and weather the storm.

We have arrived at a time when if you can't touch it, you don't own it. Hold your own wealth in a private secure place. Protect yourself.

Chapter *14*
What Are You Waiting For?
Carpe Diem...Seize The Day

We go forward from here. Studies of what has happened up to this point in history are only useful insofar as they can be of assistance in the understanding of where we are now and where the various forks in the road ahead will take us. To some of those who may read this book it has been nothing but a painfully tiresome restating of the obvious. To others, it is pure fantasy, and is destined to be discarded. To others still, it may be the first clear picture that they have ever had, that ties together all of the bothersome snags that have puzzled them about the unraveling fabric of society. In the end though, even the most accurate, timely, clear, and reliable warning is useless if it is ignored.

Every individual must make up their own mind. It is the hearty recommendation of the authors that questions that have arisen, or may arise in the reader's mind, about any and all aspects of the glimpse of things offered here should be researched further. Any honest seeker of truth may have contrary opinions to those expressed in this book. That is fine, as long as their opinions are based upon evidence, not inarguable belief. Truth is often rendered inert and useless when hampered by prejudicial belief that negates all evidence and withstands all valid challenge or reasoning. If it is truly a matter of opinion, then time and the mushrooming reality of what is coming will ultimately persuade.

Verification never hurts, but it must be understood and truly sink in that it should be done expeditiously. Too much time should not be spent at it, as time is not on our side. Now is already past the moment for action.

The picture painted in these pages of the times upon us may be difficult for some to agree with, but the facts about the decline in available silver which make it the investment of the age are starkly visible and therefore quite simple to verify. *In the hypothetical possibility that the events of the future bear no resemblance to the view put forward here, the prudence of silver as an investment is still obvious.* **The Silver Bomb** will go off and when it does, those that have heeded the advice in this book will be very glad for it. Those that have not will be doubly sorry. First that it occurred, and second that they were given, if not ample, then sufficient warning, but took no action. It would have been no better for them than to have been left in the dark.

It is our brightest hope that you have found this book to be helpful and that it has provided some benefit to you. We hope you enjoyed reading it as well. We hope it will make you think about where we are in history and about the future we are all facing. We hope most of all that it gave you some concrete ideas about how you may get positioned for the future in order to benefit from it, not be bludgeoned by it.

May God bless you, your family and our world.

With our sincerest thanks,

Michael & Christopher

Appendix

Visit the official website for **The Silver Bomb** at: http://thesilverbomb.com/.

Feel free to just browse the site from time to time for news and fresh articles, or log in to be able to leave comments or interact with other readers on the blog page. There are lots of like-minded people who would love to exchange ideas with you.

Frequently Asked Questions:

1. What preparations should I consider for a financial collapse? http://www.wholesalegoldgroup.com/investing-in-gold-silver-frequently-asked-questions/top-10-things-you-can-do-to-prepare-for-economic-collapse

2. What does the Bible say about silver and gold? http://www.wholesalegoldgroup.com/investing-in-gold-silver-frequently-asked-questions/what-does-the-bible-say-about-gold-and-silver

3. What are some coin grades and definitions? http://www.wholesalegoldgroup.com/investing-in-gold-silver-frequently-asked-questions/coin-grades-defined

The Silver Bomb

Value of a $1 Federal Reserve Note in 1913 Dollars
(Source: US Bureau of Labor Statistics)

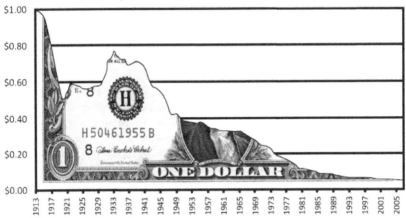